Strategic FUEL for Nonprofits

Most nonprofits approach strategic planning in ways that take too much time and effort, focus on the wrong issues, and set up the plan to be something that gathers dust on a shelf rather than being implemented. If you want a different approach, this is the book for you.

This book shows nonprofit leaders and organizations how to conduct strategic planning processes that deliver both a great strategy and an organization that can drive strategic change and continually refresh its strategy. It introduces a new framework—Strategic FUEL—and shows leaders how to map their organization's strategic situation to a planning approach that addresses the most important opportunities and challenges, without wasting time and effort. It also shows the actions leaders can take during strategic planning to increase the odds of successful strategy implementation. The core content of this book was developed while working with nonprofit leaders on strategic planning, so it converts the best research and ideas to practice and step-by-step guidance.

This book will be a valuable resource for nonprofit CEOs and their teams, foundations looking to support their nonprofit grantees, and students in nonprofit management courses and programs. While the book is focused on the nonprofit world, the lessons are also applicable to any leader trying to drive strategy effectively.

Charles Moore is the CEO of Thrive Street Advisors and a trusted advisor and strategy consultant to nonprofit and for-profit leaders. He is an adjunct faculty member at the Georgetown Center for Public & Nonprofit Leadership and has served on the boards Father's Uplift, EdFuel, SchoolTalk, and Monument Academy. Charles holds a bachelor's degree in Economics from Harvard and an MBA and master's degree in Education from Stanford.

"Good strategy for uncertain environments, I've always suspected, should be more "search algorithm" than 'itinerary.' In this book, Charles provides a compelling plan for organizing around that principle, full of hard-won wisdom on how to rally your team to make it happen."

Paul Niehaus, Ph.D., Founder, Give Directly

"As much as we might want a strategy to be 'done' and crossed off our to-do lists, it must constantly evolve to deliver value. This book offers an insightful framework for elevating your organization's approach to strategy and keeping it relevant."

Clarence Wardell III, Ph.D., Senior Program Officer, Gates Foundation

Strategic FUEL for Nonprofits

How to Create a Strategy That Is Focused, Understandable, Embedded, and Living

Charles Moore

Routledge
Taylor & Francis Group

NEW YORK AND LONDON

Designed cover image: Getty

First published 2025
by Routledge
605 Third Avenue, New York, NY 10158

and by Routledge
4 Park Square, Milton Park, Abingdon, Oxon OX14 4RN

Routledge is an imprint of the Taylor & Francis Group, an informa business

Library of Congress Cataloging-in-Publication Data
A catalog record for this title has been requested

ISBN: 978-1-032-81390-5 (hbk)
ISBN: 978-1-032-81273-1 (pbk)
ISBN: 978-1-003-49961-9 (ebk)

DOI: 10.4324/9781003499619

Typeset in Galliard
by Taylor & Francis Books

This work is dedicated to all those who labor to create a better world.

Contents

Illustrations

Figures

Acknowledgments

Thanks to you, the reader, for taking the time to read and engage with this book. Your interest, feedback, and support make writing a truly rewarding experience.

This book required the contributions of many people.

Thanks to the colleagues and friends who shared their experiences and provided feedback as I developed and refined the ideas for this book. They include Amir Ali, Anne Marie Burgoyne, Lindsey Cooksen, Mary Kate Cunningham, Abby Davidson, Rick DeJarnette, Kevin Dowdell, Suzanne Ehlers, Erin Fiaschetti, Erin Frackleton, Adriane Gamble, Natalie Guillen, Alix Guerrier, Tara Hofmann, Monica Hopkins, Steph Itelman, Roshni Jain, Brooke Jones, Justina Lai, Simmons Lettre, Mark Lockwood, David Osei, Bisi Oyedele, Mason Pan, Amit Patel, Erica Phillips, Jacqui Purcell, Guilia Salieri, Shalini Shybut, Liz Simmons, Norm Smith, Spencer Smith, Rebecca Taber Staehelin, Jonathan Tate, Aoife Toomey, Anika Warren Wood, David Williamson, and Jessica Wodatch.

Thanks to those brave and generous souls who read rough—sometimes, really rough—drafts. I appreciate their candor, encouragement, and thought partnership in refining the core ideas. These folks include Jessica Bieligk, Martha Blue, Noah Eisenkraft, Lauren Hult, Melissa Kessler, Kofi Kumi, Gerard McGeary, Garrett Ulosevich, Jeremy Utley, and Clarence Wardell.

Thanks to this book's editorial and publication team for their guidance, artful nudges to keep going, and for helping me sound like a reasonably intelligent person who paid attention to grammar lessons in grade school. The team includes Trisha Giramma, Maura Grace Harrington Logue, Bethany Nelson, Meredith Norwich, and Kammy Wood.

Finally, thanks to my wife, Erin, for indulging the effort and giving grace for the evening and weekend writing sessions.

Thank you all for your invaluable contributions and for making this book possible.

About the Author

Charles Moore is a trusted advisor and consultant to nonprofit, for-profit, and government leaders.

Charles was trained in the art and science of strategy during two stints at McKinsey & Company and continues this work as CEO of Thrive Street Advisors. He has supported dozens of organizations in improving performance, including strategy efforts at nearly twenty nonprofits.

As an executive coach, Charles has worked with over eighty nonprofit Executive Directors and business executives on their challenges in leading effectively and driving strategic change. His clients have worked for some of the world's leading organizations like Amazon, Google, Capital One, Hilton Hotels, and the U.S. Senate.

Charles has served on the boards of the nonprofits Father's Uplift and EdFuel, and he has been the Board Chair of SchoolTalk and Monument Academy Public Charter School. Charles has taught Change Management as an adjunct faculty member at the Georgetown Center for Public & Nonprofit Leadership.

Charles holds a bachelor's degree in Economics from Harvard and earned an MBA from Stanford, with a certificate in Public Management. He also holds a master's degree in Education from Stanford. Charles lives in Washington, D.C. with his wife, Erin, and two kids, who are continually charged up.

Introduction

Strategic Planning Doesn't Necessarily Lead to Strategic Impact. That's Why You Need Strategic FUEL

THE PROBLEM WITH MOST STRATEGIC PLANNING PROCESSES

Imagine you are driving a bus from New York City to Los Angeles. Everyone in your organization is on board.

If this were 2002, you would probably enter the destination in MapQuest and print the turn-by-turn instructions. You would probably also plot out where to stop on the road, and where to stay overnight. With limited access to the internet, you would probably stick with the plan until you got to the destination.

Traffic jam? Well, you're stuck.

What's more, only you and *maybe* a capable navigator in the front seat know where the bus is headed. Everyone else is just along for the ride, and all they know is the updates and information you provide for them during the trip.

Now imagine taking that same trip today. You still identify a specific destination but enter it into Waze or a similar app, providing ongoing, real-time scanning of the environment and the path ahead. As soon as the app sees a traffic jam, it looks for a way around it. And everyone on the bus can access all the information you know—and maybe more, since they're not driving. If they know how to reach the destination and feel comfortable contributing ideas, they can help make the trip faster, more enjoyable, or both.

Strategic planning is much like this road trip. Unfortunately, most nonprofits' processes are stuck in the 2002 version—plotting every single step upfront, with no ability to deviate from the plan and one-way communication with passengers.

An effective strategic planning process should be more like the modern road trip. Rather than just identifying the destination, it should also be about creating an organization able to collectively plot the journey to that destination. It should also equip the organization to learn and adapt as external factors change.

This book was created to help you design and run a strategic planning process that delivers not only a new plan but a new, more enduring way of working on strategy.

DOI: 10.4324/9781003499619-1

THE ASPIRATION: CONDUCT A STRATEGIC PLANNING PROCESS THAT BUILDS STRATEGIC FUEL

I regularly talk to leaders who are considering a strategic planning effort. In those conversations, I usually ask questions like:

What do customers say when you ask them for feedback about what they value most in the service? What else do they want from you?

For what specific reasons do customers choose you over competitors?

Can you show me the last few quarterly employee surveys that indicate what the employees need from the organization?

Unfortunately, their answers to those questions often leave me wanting. When leaders do not have good answers to those questions, it is usually a sign their organization has accidentally stopped strategizing. Sure, there's a stated strategy, but it is unlikely to have been refreshed with feedback and learning.

The alternative to that state is building and sustaining Strategic FUEL, which helps your organization keep its strategy fresh and relevant.

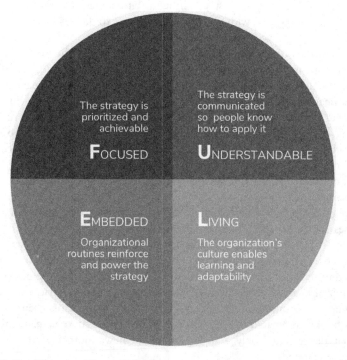

Figure I.I The Elements of Strategic FUEL

In the body, metabolism is the process by which the body converts the fuel of food and drink into energy. When we have high-quality fuel and efficient conversion, we have the energy to achieve our goals.

In strategy, the high-quality fuel comes from consuming ideas from outside of the organization and understanding the needs of customers and other stakeholders. That creates a continual source of ideas for effecting strategic impact—if you build routines to do so.

That means adopting tactics like:

- Having an always-on conversation with those you serve, employees, and external stakeholders to understand best what they want from you
- Leaving the office to see operations and customers firsthand so that ideas do not get overly filtered before they reach the senior team
- Developing an inclusive operating model in which those who directly talk to customers and understand their needs are also directly involved in the strategy conversation

The "efficient conversion" in strategy comes from all of the processes that help the organization turn those ideas and insights into action. For the most strategic organizations, these are embedded in organizational routines. That's what helps those organizations be truly dynamic.

When I was a kid, my sister and I would spend several weeks each summer with my grandparents in Selma, Alabama. Unfortunately, my grandfather—the first Charles Moore—didn't believe in using air conditioning, even as the temperatures reached *oppressive* levels, and he'd turn on the oven and stove at 3:00 p.m. to cook dinner. His instruction to deal with the stifling environment was to "let up the window."

Strategic FUEL is fundamentally about helping your organization let up the windows, enable the fresh air of ideas to come in and circulate, and keep its strategy dynamic and relevant as a result.

BUILDING STRATEGIC FUEL REQUIRES A DIFFERENT PLANNING PROCESS

Strategic planning does not automatically deliver impact. The impact comes from a process in which stakeholders grapple with the opportunities and challenges the organization faces and, with that understanding, proactively choose to move forward together.

That is why a process that aims to generate Strategic FUEL focuses on creating productive debate and alignment, and building internal capabilities at each step.

Here's how your experience of planning is different with this approach:

Typical Strategic Planning	Building Strategic FUEL
Consultants conduct focus groups and write a report about what they heard	You and other leaders conduct authentic dialogues with your teams, enabling everyone to feel heard and respected
Consultants conduct "interviews" with external stakeholders to get information and perspectives from them	You hold authentic, two-way conversations with stakeholders to build stronger ongoing institutional relationships
Leaders hold special "strategic planning meetings" to build the strategy	You build strategic thinking into ongoing organizational routines
Planning committees focus on building consensus, which can result in watered-down or confusing strategy	You create a *healthy debate* that helps people wrestle with the challenges and make clear strategic choices
Leaders develop a "rollout plan" for communicating the final strategy	You create an ongoing dialogue in which leaders share what they are learning, share emerging strategy ideas, and ask for feedback. By the end of the planning process, everyone understands both the *what* and the *why* of the strategy
The organization waits until next year (or five years from now) to engage strategy questions again	You continue to evolve the strategy as you learn so that it is always relevant

When a team uses the planning process to practice new ways of working together and starts to build strategy into its existing organizational routines, it is set up for greater success. These are not mere "implementation" issues to shoehorn at the end of the planning process. Indeed, they are central to creating a more strategic organization.

In this approach, the consultant plays a support role like a fitness trainer—i.e., facilitating, coaching, and training team members where relevant—but the organization's leaders have to lift the weights.

If you're doing the work well, you shouldn't have to hire a consultant next time!

THE GOOD NEWS: WHEN YOU HAVE STRATEGIC FUEL, LEADING YOUR ORGANIZATION IS EASIER

Strategic FUEL is about helping the entire organization be great at learning and strategy, which lightens the load on senior leaders. In his book *The Fifth Discipline*, Peter Senge writes about how vital this is. "As the world becomes more interconnected and business becomes more complex and dynamic, work must become more 'learningful.'"[1] He continues, "The organizations that will truly excel in the future will be the organizations that discover how to tap people's commitment and capacity to learn at all levels in an organization."[2]

As you implement this approach, you'll likely find that it:

- Helps you create greater ongoing alignment in the organization (and spend less time dealing with the consequences of misalignment)
- Helps you build a culture in which more people understand the need for change and willingly pursue it
- Helps junior leaders develop strategic skills, which puts them in a position to take on more senior roles
- Helps you not have to carry strategy alone

THE CORE ARGUMENTS OF THIS BOOK

1 Most nonprofits approach strategic planning in ways that take too much time and effort, with uncertain impact

As a consultant, I regularly read nonprofits' requests for proposal (RFPs) for creating a three- or five-year strategic plan. Too often, my reaction is, "These folks are about to waste a lot of time and money on a long document with fancy words that never gets used."

The first giveaway is that the RFP lists requirements for the project that reads like the "Steps in the Process" section from a Wikipedia page on strategic planning. But the most important sign of a potentially wasteful process is when there's no clear sense of the opportunities the organization wants to pursue or the challenges it most needs to address. Often, *our last plan was five years ago* is the primary motivating factor. A process based on that rationale is likely to create a confusing strategy.

If that's your motivation, you can close this book now.

This book will help you design a planning process that directly addresses the most important opportunities and challenges—with the right amount of effort.

2 The BIG PROCESS approach to strategic planning is a good way to manage the politics of setting strategy. It will help you find an acceptable answer, but it does not always help you find the right strategic answer

Strategic planning is inherently a political act. That's not to say that the "right answer" does not matter—just that the "right answer" is subjective, even if you have the best analysis. All the strategic steps after that analysis—e.g., setting priorities, generating buy-in, adjusting the organization's budget—take political acumen to do well.

It's easy to respond to that challenge with a *big process* approach with long timelines, unwieldy committees, and consensus-based decision-making. Unfortunately, those costs do not come with guarantees of solving the political challenge or identifying the right strategic answer.

This book will help you diagnose your organization's strategic situation and show you alternatives to the time-consuming *big process* approach that also achieve better answers. If you still need the *big process* approach, this book will show you how to achieve the political aims of alignment without the downside of a confused strategy.

3 Needing to conduct a formal strategic planning process is a signal that your organization may not be strategic enough on a day-to-day basis

This book will show you how to move from a sporadic approach to strategy to a nimble, embedded approach. A process that aims to build FUEL focuses as much on building strategic capabilities as it does on identifying the right answer (which is only valid for today).

Why? If you take on planning but do not fix the organization's *ability to drive strategic change*, you'll likely find yourself in the same place three or five years from now—whenever you start the subsequent planning process.

4 If your planning process is "develop strategy, then create an implementation plan," you're wasting valuable time when you could be having an impact

Imagine trying to get in shape by researching the best workout clothes for three months. I know I've been guilty of that! Unfortunately, many strategic planning processes are conducted this way.

The approach you'll read here will help you flip the process to focus on creating the conditions for strategic change *in parallel* to getting the right answer. And it will show you how to move into action as quickly as possible.

In that way, this book will help you accelerate impact, which I suspect you most care about anyway.

5 The best strategies have a "best by" date

Setting strategy is about making informed guesses about the future. But because they are guesses and the future is uncertain, the most rigorous processes reflect that uncertainty. The plans do not *assume* the strategy will be valid for three or five years. And they do not tell everyone in the organization, "Just do this, and we'll be fine."

In this book, you will see how to set strategy in a way that helps the organization *test and iterate* as the future unfolds, which increases the likelihood that the strategy will stay relevant. You will also see how to communicate the strategy in ways that help people understand the *why*, make daily strategic choices, and be more prepared for change.

HOW I DEVELOPED A LOVE/HATE RELATIONSHIP WITH STRATEGIC PLANNING

Hi, I'm Charles Moore.

Today, I run a strategy consulting and executive coaching practice called Thrive Street Advisors. But before that, I spent my career weaving between the nonprofit and for-profit sectors and between being a consultant and a leader. This book is a synthesis of these experiences.

By way of introduction to me and to the concepts you'll read throughout this book, I want to share a few stories.

Painting the Sistine Chapel

After college, I started my career as a bright-eyed analyst at the management consulting firm McKinsey & Company. When we worked with clients, we would spend long hours trying to bring the most rigorous analysis and nuanced strategies to clients—or, at least, so I thought!

But after two years at McKinsey, I worked with the local Boys & Girls Clubs chapter. I aimed to learn the other side of strategy—actually implementing it. This is where my real education in strategy started.

I realized that developing strategy is often like painting the Sistine Chapel—a painstakingly crafted work of art. On the other hand, successfully *implementing* a strategy is like taking a kindergarten class picture—99 percent of the effort is getting everyone to look in the same direction at the same time.

Everyone, look here.

Sarah, we need everyone standing.

Tommy, turn to your left.

Your other left.

Getting everyone to look in the same direction should inform the balance of effort in the planning process. Success is generating alignment, not just getting the strategy right.

Moreover, the work to get people aligned is not a one-time task of announcing the strategy. Instead, it is about the constant effort to *keep* people looking in the same direction.

The Analysis Doesn't Always Matter

The other thing I learned in my stint at Boys & Girls Clubs is the limited power of analysis.

One of our big strategic projects was understanding how we might better allocate the Clubs around the region. The long and short of it: several neighborhoods with Clubs had experienced rapid gentrification, meaning fewer underprivileged kids lived around them. It also meant that the land beneath the clubs became one of the organization's most significant financial assets.

We hired a consultant to help us analyze the issue. We formed a committee of the board of directors to study it. We wrote a lengthy report with a carefully reasoned conclusion that we should try to redevelop the land to access the asset value *and* build brand new Clubs for the kids who still lived in those gentrifying neighborhoods. It was a rock-solid case.

But here's the thing: No one cared. Those who understood the rationale for the change did not need to be convinced. And those who disagreed with the idea or who just did not want changes in their neighborhood would *never* be convinced.

That experience taught me that strategic change is not a function of how rigorous your strategic analysis is. Unfortunately, I have re-learned that lesson many times since then! Instead, success in strategic planning is usually a matter of understanding the barriers to change—both logical and emotional—and addressing those in a savvy way. It is intrinsically a leadership and political exercise.

That insight also means the pace and effort of planning is driven by the problem you are trying to solve. There are techniques you can use to develop strategic insights rapidly. There are situations in which the "planning" phase need not last more than a few days or weeks, and the action phase can start immediately. And there are situations where you need less time from expensive consultants and way more time from the organization's leaders.

You'll read more about that in this book.

Having a Split Personality

After working at Boys & Girls Clubs, I decamped to California to attend business school at Stanford. Given my long-standing interest in education and the nonprofit sector, I also enrolled in the education school there.

Being in both environments simultaneously created a sometimes strange experience. Among my business school friends, I was a touchy-feely nonprofit guy. And while at education school, people sometimes thought of me as one of those hard-core businesspeople who did not get the human-centered enterprise that is helping kids succeed.

Turns out, I'm the same person.

Most importantly, when studying the for-profit and nonprofit sectors, I saw that we were working on the same issues—just using different language.

After graduate school, I similarly straddled the sectors when I returned to McKinsey, later worked at Capital One, and served on several nonprofit boards. I had the same feeling. The goals are different, but the challenges of getting a group of humans to achieve ambitious goals are essentially the same.

When I once worked with the board and leadership team of a local charter school, the CEO of the school remarked, "We could achieve breakthrough outcomes if it weren't for all of the drama on the team!" I asked, "Have you ever experienced an environment where that *wasn't* the case?"

Having conducted almost forty consulting engagements across the for-profit, nonprofit, and government sectors, I assure you that dynamic exists in every. single. organization.

Along the way, I got trained as an executive coach. Since then, I have done nearly 700 hours of executive coaching, including for ten nonprofit executive directors and over twenty-five vice president-level and C-suite executives. That gave me even more of a window into the challenges these executives face in driving strategic change in their organizations—the technical, the political, and the interpersonal. The work is hard for everyone!

All of that experience is why this book focuses so much on solving the human challenges of doing strategy well. This book will not only talk about how to take on the process, but it will help you think about doing strategic planning in a way that achieves impact.

Resolving the Love/Hate Relationship

If I have a love/hate relationship with strategic planning, why do I continue to do it? Why write this book?

I hate spending time on analysis that does not matter, which led me to develop tools to identify what analyses *do* matter.

I hate doing external stakeholder interviews and employee surveys and thinking, "This organization is spending a lot of money to have me do something they should do for themselves on a regular basis." So, I wrote this book to help you build internal capabilities and robust ongoing routines.

I hate developing a strategic plan for an organization and knowing that they'll be stuck in three or five years because they don't have the team capacity to keep the strategy fresh. That's why this book is built around Strategic FUEL and urges you to focus on building strategic capabilities from the *start* of the process.

When an organization is so in tune with clients, employees, and external stakeholders that it continually meets their needs, I love it.

When an organization has the ability to continually reflect on and adjust its strategy such that they don't need my help, I love that.

When their strategy is so embedded in their day-to-day work that they don't even need a process called "strategic planning," that's when I absolutely love strategic planning.

This book is my strategic planning love letter to you.

BEFORE WE GET STARTED, A NOTE ON LANGUAGE

This book is written for nonprofit leaders, but when reading an early draft of it, a nonprofit leader said, "I notice that you include a lot of business examples. Is it your argument that nonprofit strategy is the same as for-profit strategy?"

After thinking about it briefly, I said, "Basically, yes."

It is worth stipulating that every sector and industry has unique strategy dynamics. How technology companies compete to win in cloud computing vastly differs from how nonprofits "compete" for their clients, employees, and donors. Similarly, a nonprofit running a soup kitchen will have different strategic concerns than a nonprofit running schools, as their funding and operational models differ substantially.

But despite those technical differences, my experience is that the core ideas of strategy and the *human experience* of setting strategy are similar across sectors.

First, every organization should have a clear purpose and a crisp definition of success. Still, many organizations and teams, regardless of sector, struggle to keep their purpose and strategic vision front of mind. It is easy for everyone to get caught up in their day-to-day to-do lists, what their colleagues want from them, and organizational politics—everything happening *today* and everything *inside* the organization. This is a phenomenon of humans and groups, not specifically a function of the sector.

Moreover, nearly every organization struggles with keeping its "customers" at the center of its work. When I talk to nonprofit leaders, the language of "customers" does not always resonate. That's partly because it has a commercial ring to it and partly because nonprofits have multiple stakeholders—the people they serve, the people who fund them, and the larger community they are trying to improve with their services.

But it's worth thinking with a customer lens for this simple reason: If the people you need to join the effort have a choice, then it's worth understanding what matters to them and how they will make that choice.

This applies equally to those you serve, donors, and critical suppliers.

For all those reasons, throughout this book, you will see examples and language from the nonprofit and for-profit sectors. The terms "CEO," "executive director," and "top leader" are interchangeable. "Customers" and "clients" are both used for the people who consume your organization's product or service.

HOW TO READ THIS BOOK

Strategic FUEL for Nonprofits is written for senior leaders who want to plot a different course for their organizations.

In the next chapter, you'll see the four elements of Strategic FUEL. The rest of the book is organized around those elements—the first two help you navigate a strategic planning process, and the latter two help you build effective strategy routines and culture. You can read all of it at once, but the book is designed to be consumed in small chunks. I know you're busy!

Let's go!

Notes

1 Peter Senge, *The Fifth Discipline: The Art and Practice of the Learning Organization* (New York: Crown Business, 2006), 14, e-book.
2 Ibid.

References

Peter Senge, *The Fifth Discipline: The Art and Practice of the Learning Organization* (New York: Crown Business, 2006), 14, e-book.

Chapter 1

The Elements of Strategic FUEL

If I'm going to argue that you should take a different approach to strategy than you are probably using now, I figured it would be helpful to outline the reasons why.

In this chapter, you will see the four elements of Strategic FUEL, why each is important, questions to help you assess how your organization is doing, and how you can start to build them during your strategic planning process.

ELEMENT 1: THE STRATEGY IS FOCUSED

I own exactly one pair of jeans.

About 90 percent of my clothes are from just two stores—I never see a need to complicate the search process.

And my kids live under a household rule that if they don't put their toys away at the end of the night, there's a good chance they'll be in the trash or Goodwill bin by the morning. It's a harsh rule, but it keeps the house tidy!

DOI: 10.4324/9781003499619-2

Long story short: I like to keep things simple. When there are fewer things cluttering my space, mind, and to-do list, it is much easier to make progress on the things that matter most.

Beyond my personal affinity for simplicity and focus, it is one of the most important parts of effective strategy. For example, in the book *In Search of Excellence*, strategy consultants Tom Peters and Robert Waterman write, "One of the key attributes of the excellent companies is that they have realized the importance of keeping things simple despite overwhelming genuine pressures to complicate things."[1]

In a completely different context, the former head of the U.S. Special Operations Command, Admiral William McRaven, wrote a master's thesis on what allows a smaller military force to defeat a larger one. One of the six components was having a plan that limits "the number of tactical objectives to only those that are vital."[2]

Why is focus so important for strategy?

In the book *Unleashed*, Harvard Business School professor Frances Frei and scholar Anne Morriss write that a major lesson of their research "is that organizations that resist and try to be great at everything usually end up in a state of 'exhausted mediocrity.'"[3]

Nonprofit work is already hard enough—there's no need to set yourself up for exhaustion and mediocrity.

In the case of special operations, there are two benefits of focus that are relevant for any team. The military reason to limit the number of objectives is to achieve "relative superiority" where it matters most. You squander this advantage by spreading resources thin.[4] Moreover, McRaven's research shows that limiting objectives focuses the training and "decreases the number of 'moving parts.'"[5]

Those benefits are relevant to teams in all contexts because they are related to the fact that it is humans who are coordinating the moving parts. If your organization has humans, you need a focused strategy!

Does Your Organization Currently Have a Focused Strategy?

The prompts below contain the elements of a focused strategy. As you read through the prompts, answer *Yes, No,* or *I Don't Know*.

1 The organization has a clear mission statement.
2 The organization has a clear vision of the impact it seeks to make (e.g., offering what, to whom, for what purpose).
3 The organization has defined the critical steps to reach that vision or strategic destination.
4 The organization has identified programs or services, customer segments, and activities that fall *outside* of the vision and is willing to sacrifice them to focus on the most critical areas.

5   The organization has defined the most important capabilities required to reach the strategic destination.

6   The organization has identified capabilities where it is willing to be mediocre or even weak in order to concentrate attention and resources on the most important capabilities.

7   The current strategy directly addresses the most critical challenges or impediments to success.

8   The organization has an economic model that enables it to achieve its vision and be reasonably sustainable going forward.

If you answered *Yes* to almost all the questions above, your organization likely has a focused strategy. Of course, having a focused strategy does not necessarily mean the current strategy is optimal for the future. However, having clarity on the strategy helps you better identify where it needs to be altered or evolved to be more effective.

If there are elements for which you answered *No* or *I Don't Know*, a helpful first step would be for you and each member of the leadership team to write down the current strategy. The conversation will likely surface insights on where the challenges are and where the team is aligned or misaligned.

Creating a Focused Strategy Requires a Planning Process Designed to Achieve It

Several years ago, I helped a small nonprofit law firm develop its strategy. We conducted a survey of its board and staff that included this question: *To have greater impact, what should the organization be doing that it is not doing currently?*
Eighteen of the twenty-one respondents had an answer to that question.

But in response to the question, *What is one program or activity the organization does today that may have outlived its usefulness?*—a soft version of asking *What should we subtract to be more focused?*—only two people who completed the survey had a concrete suggestion. Most others did not answer or were not sure.

Of course, few people object to the idea that focus and prioritization are important—they are just hard to do in reality.

The first step toward greater prioritization is to provide explicit prompts for people to consider subtraction as they explore strategy. *What should we start doing?* and *What should we stop doing?*

You can also set arbitrary limits for how many significant initiatives to take on in the new strategy. Arbitrary limits are a blunt tool, but they help force choices about what's most important to do and what's nice to have. Whenever I have seen it, the conversation about whether Project #5 or Project #6 is more important only happens when a rule limits the group to just five projects. Without limits, prioritization is just theoretical.

The important part of taking these steps during the planning process is that they mirror the mindsets and behaviors that help the organization maintain a focused strategy during the implementation.

ELEMENT 2: THE STRATEGY IS UNDERSTANDABLE

It's not enough to merely have a strategy. People in the organization need to understand and believe in it to make progress.

That's why a focused strategy must be paired with leaders' clear communication about it. Because human beings need to coordinate to implement strategy effectively, it must be simplified for consumption, regardless of its complexity.

Unfortunately, many organizations do not communicate about strategy effectively. In *Unleashed*, Frei and Morriss write: "This scale of leadership depends on people understanding the strategy well enough to inform their own decisions with it. In our experience, too many companies are held back by strategic confusion below the most senior ranks."[6]

Instead of conveying simple and effective messages, leaders' communications are often filled with jargon and fancy talk. Chip and Dan Heath, professors at Stanford and Duke, respectively, put this well in their book *Made to Stick*: "To a CEO, 'maximizing shareholder value' may be an immensely useful rule of behavior. To a flight attendant, it's not."[7]

Many strategic planning processes leave communication until...you know, there's a strategy. So why mention it now? The foundation of effective communication happens *throughout* the process as you enable people to wrestle with the case for change.

Later, I'll provide more specific guidance on creating a "Strategic Principle" and a "Focusing Question" to guide this simple communication. The main point here is that the planning process should be oriented toward finding the messages that enable stakeholders to understand their role in the strategy.

How Effective Is Your Strategy Communication?

As you read through the prompts, answer *Yes, No,* or *I Don't Know.*

1. The average person in our organization could articulate the strategy.
2. The average person in our organization consciously uses the strategy to guide their day-to-day efforts (e.g., decide what's most important to work on).

If you answered *No* or *I Don't Know* to either prompt, there is an opportunity to improve how the strategy is delivered to or consumed by people in the organization.

ELEMENT 3: THE STRATEGY IS EMBEDDED

How is the organization doing?
What's most important to accomplish?
What changes should we make to achieve those important objectives?

These questions are the heart of strategy.

The most strategic organizations ask themselves those questions continually—in fact, they are the heart of every organizational routine. They're discussed in the weekly team meeting. The questions are visited when teams review client feedback. They even come up in budget review meetings!

Indeed, the annual strategy process is only distinct for the most strategic organizations because they ask those questions with a longer time horizon.

By continually investing in their flexibility and creativity, organizations can respond to external events and refresh their strategy. When an organization has the proper routines, it becomes more effective by:

- **Learning more rapidly.** Routines encourage (or require!) people to reflect regularly on their work and how the system is operating so they can identify better paths forward.
- **Focusing talent more effectively.** When organizations proactively move the right people to the right work (i.e., where they can make the most impact), they can achieve more significant results.
- **Focusing attention.** Leaders can use routines to shape how people define success and what mental models and questions they can use to drive independent actions. This encourages everyone to engage in actions that better align with the organization's overall strategy.
- **Focusing financial resources.** Many organizations set a budget once per year, but a more proactive and ongoing reallocation of resources to the right activities is a critical factor in aligning action to the organization's overall strategy.

Does Strategy Live in Your Organization's Routines?

The prompts below will help you consider your organization's ability to learn and evolve strategy—i.e., to be strategic. As you read the prompts, answer *Yes, No,* or *I Don't Know.*

1 We regularly solicit feedback from the people we serve about what they value most (and least) about our programs and services.
2 We regularly solicit employees' feedback about their experience and how we can improve things for them.
3 We regularly solicit feedback from partners, donors, and other external stakeholders about how well we're doing and how we can improve.
4 When we learn something—from within or outside—we are good at sharing the lessons across the organization.
5 We have routines that help us identify the most important activities, and then we follow through on that prioritization.

The more you answered *Yes* to the prompts above, the more likely your organization has the raw ingredients to enable your strategy to evolve.

ELEMENT 4: THE STRATEGY IS LIVING

Strategy is just today's best guess about the future—an educated guess, sure, but a guess nonetheless. Moreover, the quality of that guess is inherently limited by the information the team has when setting the strategy.

The most strategic organizations recognize this dynamic. Rather than treating their strategies as if they are written on stone tablets, these organizations continually test their assumptions and update their strategies as they learn.

In those organizations, people do things like:

- Constantly seek new information
- Robustly debate ideas in the spirit of allowing the best information to drive solutions
- Proactively surface the organization's challenges to enable open discussion of solutions
- Continually reallocate resources from activities whose impact has decreased to those activities believed to have the highest impact in the future

This is what it means to have a living strategy. A living strategy is part of the lifeblood of how the team operates.

A living strategy refreshes itself.

A living strategy is a learning strategy.

Unfortunately, the actions that enable the organization's strategy to adapt also require individuals to show vulnerability, and our human instincts tell us to do the exact opposite. In *The Fearless Organization*, Harvard professor Amy Edmondson describes why people hold back to avoid being negatively judged at work. She writes, "Our image is perpetually at risk. At any moment, we might come across as ignorant, incompetent, or intrusive, if we do such things as ask questions, admit mistakes, offer ideas, or criticize a plan."[8]

Strategy is both an intellectual and emotional pursuit. An organization can have a great strategy, but it will never be great *at* strategy unless the culture makes it safe for people to have robust debates and to change their minds when conditions require doing so. That should sound like:

That initiative was a good idea when we started, but if I were to focus our energy on the highest impact work today, I'd do this other initiative instead.

That pilot helped us learn a lot about our customers. We'll end the pilot, but we'll integrate those lessons to strengthen our other products.

My old answer was good, but this new one is even more right.

Creating such a culture takes time, but it's vital for enabling the strategy to remain focused and relevant rather than unwieldy and stale.

How Strategic Is Your Organization's Culture?

To quickly understand whether the culture supports strategic learning and adaptation, answer *Yes, No,* or *I Don't Know* to the prompts below.

1   People feel comfortable sharing their challenges and performance shortfalls in public settings.
2   Leaders of departments proactively and openly end projects that are not working well or not working as expected.
3   When there's an error or mistake, we study it openly, without placing blame.
4   People regularly tell me, as a leader, bad news and ask for help *before* it becomes a severe problem.

The more you answered *Yes* to the prompts above, the more likely your organization can evolve its strategy over time. Regardless of your strategic planning approach and what strategy your organization pursues, this is a critical capability to achieve the impact you desire.

KEY TAKEAWAYS

1 The four elements of Strategic FUEL:

- Focused: The strategy is prioritized and achievable
- Understandable: The strategy is communicated so people know how to apply it
- Embedded: Organizational routines reinforce and power the strategy
- Living: The organization's culture enables learning and adaptability

2 An organization can have a great strategy, but it will never be great at strategy unless it addresses all four elements.
3 The work to create a more strategic organization should start at the beginning of strategic planning rather than waiting until implementation.

ENGAGE YOUR TEAM

Visit the book website to download the Bonus Resources, which contains a printable version of the questions under each element of Strategic FUEL. Engaging your team on those questions can spur action toward building a more strategic organization.

www.thrivestreetadvisors.com/strategic-fuel-for-nonprofits

WHAT'S NEXT

The rest of this book is organized around the four elements of Strategic FUEL. The first two elements are what most people think of as strategic planning—developing and communicating the strategy. However, the organization's ability to do something with the strategy requires the routines and culture of the final two elements.

All four components of Strategic FUEL are part of a holistic system to drive progress. The elements represent a multiplication problem—when one factor is zero, it risks slowing overall strategic progress to zero. That's why you should address all of the elements in parallel. In the next section, you will see how to design a planning process that helps you do so.

Notes

1 Thomas Peters and Robert Waterman, Jr, *In Search of Excellence: Lessons from America's Best-Run Companies* (New York: HarperCollins, 2012), 63, e-book.
2 William McRaven, "The Theory of Special Operations" (Master's thesis, Naval Postgraduate Institute, 1993).
3 Frances Frei and Anne Morriss, *Unleashed: The Unapologetic Leader's Guide to Empowering Everyone Around You* (Boston, MA: Harvard Business Review Press, 2020), 126, e-book.
4 McRaven (1993).
5 Ibid, 18.
6 Frei and Morriss (2020), 125.
7 Chip Heath and Dan Heath, *Made to Stick: Why Some Ideas Survive and Others Die* (New York: Random House, 2007), 57, e-book.

8 Amy Edmondson, *The Fearless Organization: Creating Psychological Safety in the Workplace for Learning, Innovation, and Growth* (Hoboken, NJ: Wiley, 2019), 13, e-book.

References

Amy Edmondson, *The Fearless Organization: Creating Psychological Safety in the Workplace for Learning, Innovation, and Growth* (Hoboken, NJ: Wiley, 2019), 13, e-book.
Frances Frei and Anne Morriss, *Unleashed: The Unapologetic Leader's Guide to Empowering Everyone Around You* (Boston, MA: Harvard Business Review Press, 2020), 126, e-book.
Chip Heath and Dan Heath, *Made to Stick: Why Some Ideas Survive and Others Die* (New York: Random House, 2007), 57, e-book.
William McRaven, "The Theory of Special Operations" (Master's thesis, Naval Postgraduate Institute, 1993).
Thomas Peters and Robert Waterman, Jr, *In Search of Excellence: Lessons from America's Best-Run Companies* (New York: HarperCollins, 2012), 63, e-book.

Designing a Planning Process That Generates Strategic FUEL

Chapter 2

Determining What Strategic Planning Approach Your Organization Needs

Why are you doing strategic planning?

Seriously, take a moment to consider that question.

The *why* question is the first thing I ask leaders when they are thinking about strategic planning. If they do not give a direct answer to that question, I usually probe more. *Is there a strategic challenge you're attempting to solve or an opportunity you're going after?*

A colleague told me her go-to question for leaders considering strategic planning is this: *Is there a specific decision you need to make?*

The reason you should push yourself to identify a crisp rationale for strategic planning is that it is often a long, time-consuming process, and there is no guarantee that the effort will yield a meaningfully improved strategy or enable you to make critical decisions in front of the organization with more rigor.

Rather than conducting a generic planning process, you should design the process to fit your organization's strategic situation. Doing so increases the odds that the process will address the correct issues and consume only the time and resources necessary.

WHAT STRATEGY SITUATION DOES YOUR ORGANIZATION FACE?

In this section, you will find descriptions of several generic strategy situations. As you read through the situations, consider their relevance to your organization.

By identifying the most relevant strategy situations, you'll be able to home in on the most important strategic questions to answer during your organization's strategic planning process. This is important to ensure that your team's efforts are focused appropriately.

DOI: 10.4324/9781003499619-4

Strategy Situations

A New Opportunity

We've been offered a new opportunity—e.g., potential new funding or a merger or acquisition offer—and we need to decide what to do. Because the opportunity was unexpected, the team likely has not fully reasoned through the implications.

B Time to Grow

We are doing well, but want to reach more people, work in new geographies, or achieve scale. To grow sustainably, we must figure out how to adjust our programs and organizational capabilities.

C We're in a Precarious Situation

The organization is in a situation that requires urgent change. A turnaround is needed, and there's little time to identify the necessary change.

D The Service or Product Isn't Cutting It

We're not delivering in a high-quality way to our clients, or what we're offering is becoming less valuable or relevant to them. This may already be visible in our growth, retention, or satisfaction scores.

E The Money Doesn't Work

We have a great service, but we're not making enough money for the organization to be sustainable. We need to change the economic model to get on a firmer footing.

F Working Here Isn't Great

We're doing great work, but the culture or how we work with each other makes the experience of working here less than ideal. This makes it harder to attract and retain talented professionals.

G Unexpected Tsunami

Forces outside our organization are creating an urgent need for us to change. We're in uncharted waters.

H Gathering Storm

Everything is mostly OK today, but we can see a storm gathering on the horizon that we must prepare for *now*. This might come from a new competitor, a technological change, or shifting priorities for customers and funders. The leadership team may already be seeing early indications of the storm, but it's not yet visible to everyone in the organization.

I Stuck in Neutral

We're stuck in our ways, or we're not getting better as an organization. We will eventually get left behind if we cannot become more dynamic.

J We're Misaligned

The departments or units of our organization are working on different strategies, are not working well together on organization-wide strategies, or are working at cross purposes.

K Out of Control

Significant growth or change in the recent past has made things feel out of control. We need to keep going in the same direction but make things feel more manageable.

L It's All Good

Of course, we can improve here or there, but we're firing on all cylinders.

M Time-Based Need to Plan

We're just updating the strategic plan because the current one is expiring. We'll probably do another three- or five-year plan, but there's no sharp edge to our thinking.

N Funder-Driven Need to Plan

We're pretty clear on the strategy—we're just doing strategic planning to have something that looks smart and interesting to funders.

MAPPING YOUR STRATEGIC SITUATION TO PLANNING APPROACH

Depending on your organization's situation, the planning process may vary in how fast, how inclusive, and how much change it entails for your core programs, products, or services. This section outlines how you might use the reflection you did earlier and identify what planning approach is most relevant to your organization.

Strategy Situation	Approach to Planning
Gathering Storm New Opportunity Time to Grow	**The BIG PROCESS Approach** Design a slower process with all of the bells and whistles and imagination of strategy. Focus on deep engagement to enable a broad understanding of the need for and implications of change.
We're in a Precarious Situation Unexpected Tsunami The Service or Product Isn't Cutting It The Money Doesn't Work	**The Focused, Tactical Problem Solving Approach** Convene cross-functional teams of experts who can design solutions directly and quickly.
Working Here Isn't Great Stuck in Neutral We're Misaligned Out of Control	**The Leadership, Routines, and Culture Approach** Take the work outside of a "strategy" framing, which can distract from the day-to-day leadership work needed for success.
It's All Good Time-Based Need to Plan Funder-Driven Need to Plan	**Consider Skipping Strategic Planning Altogether** It's probably not worth the time and effort.

The BIG PROCESS Approach

This is what most people have in mind when they think of a "strategic planning process," and it may include many of the following activities:

- Forming a cross-functional planning team that will spend months on the effort
- Conducting employee surveys and listening sessions
- Conducting extensive outreach to stakeholders
- Analyzing "competitors"
- Undertaking an inclusive, consensus-based decision-making process
- Creating a detailed implementation plan and financial model

Just reading those points is exhausting!

Going through this robust process is worthwhile when the strategy calls for substantial change—and a primary objective of the planning process is to prepare the organization for that change.

This is most relevant for the **Gathering Storm, New Opportunity**, and **Time to Grow** strategy situations. In those situations, the gathering storm, opportunity, or growth challenges are novel for people in the organization. Most people have not seen the change on the horizon or reasoned through what the change might mean for the organization. In these cases, going more slowly and being more inclusive at each step may ease the route.

Another reason to do the *big process* is because the potential change may require a deeper analysis of its impacts, and this work requires many perspectives. For example, if the question is *How do we pursue this new opportunity (e.g., program, geographic expansion, service) while keeping our existing work strong?*, having everyone who might be affected by the change share their perspectives may be critical to understanding whether the opportunity is as attractive as it seems.

Of course, all of that perspective gathering takes time—some organizations spend six to eighteen months(!) on strategic planning—so it is most relevant to those strategy situations where there is sufficient time to decide and to act.

Finally, the *big process* approach may also be relevant where external factors demand that the process appear robust and deliberate. I once worked with a nonprofit that works on affordable housing on a new five-year strategic plan. The organization had the good fortune of securing most of its revenue from government earmarks. The funding dynamic required the organization to stay within the middle-of-the-road consensus of its Congressional backers. Hence, we knew the organization's new five-year strategy would almost surely match its previous strategic plan. Bold was not an option.

But even though it could have done a copy-and-paste strategic plan, the organization had to conduct a deliberate planning process with heavy stakeholder engagement to legitimize the new plan. So, while the *big process* approach is not ideal for every strategic situation, it was a reasonable choice for that nonprofit.

Because of the time and effort involved in the *big process* approach, you should not pursue it if you can get away with other, more tailored approaches discussed in this section.

Focused, Tactical Problem Solving: The Tiger Team Approach

If the strategic challenge is evident to most people and well defined in scope, the best approach is to ask the people in your organization with the most relevant expertise to solve the challenge directly. This approach is most appropriate for **The Service or Product Isn't Cutting It, We're in a Precarious Situation**, and the **Unexpected Tsunami**.

In these situations, you need expert voices to apply the best knowledge quickly. Or, put another way, the effort to solicit a more comprehensive set of perspectives may not yield better ideas about the solution. Hence, a tiger team can be helpful.

One client, an organization that provides public defenders for those who cannot afford lawyers, adopted this approach. The organization's leaders started the strategic planning process with an instinct that a more agile, action-oriented approach would suit them.

That instinct was confirmed when its leadership team evaluated the drivers and inhibitors of progress against the previous strategic plan. A primary insight: Where they made progress were those areas that had focused attention.

Moreover, when the leadership team identified that its most critical challenge—a recent increase in employee attrition—demanded expert analysis and immediate action, it decided to experiment with tiger teams. Because the first team launched within a few weeks, they were progressing against a strategic challenge *months* before the strategic planning process was complete.

The speed advantage of tiger teams is significant when urgent action is needed. However, the key to achieving the speed benefits is that the tiger team should be almost 100 percent focused on solving the strategic challenge. This means temporarily delaying or shifting the day-to-day responsibilities of its members to others.

Finally, forming a tiger team does not mean doing the work in secret. Indeed, you may announce that the team is being created, and the team may reach out to others in the organization when additional expertise would be helpful or to get feedback on proposed solutions.

What a Tiger Team Is	
A team of experts	Because the members know the details, they can work quickly to design solutions. Membership is based on who has the expertise or perspective required to solve the specific problem, not on the representation of organizational units. However, when appropriate, the team may bring in others and solicit feedback on potential solutions.
… with a specific mandate,	Leaders define success criteria and any constraints but otherwise let the team work independently. The proposed solutions are accepted as long as they meet the success criteria.
… time and space to work synchronously,	Speed and effective problem-solving come from dedicated time and, where possible, co-location.
… and a deadline.	This is all about focused effort and action.

Bonus Resources

You will find a template for a Tiger Team Charter in the Bonus Resources available on the book website. It will help you outline its mandate and engage stakeholders.
www.thrivestreetadvisors.com/strategic-fuel-for-nonprofits

Focused, Tactical Problem Solving: The Leadership Retreat Approach

If the strategic challenge is well defined, but solving it requires a fundamentally new economic or operational model for the organization, the proper planning approach facilitates expanded thinking—i.e., a retreat. This approach is most relevant for **The Money Doesn't Work** or when a different vision for the organization is needed.

Doing this work in the form of a leadership team retreat (or series of retreats) is about removing participants from the day-to-day activities that induce them to think tactically. It is also hard to develop a new vision or model if leadership drops into an hour-long meeting, sandwiched between a budget update and solving an HR issue. The retreat enables time and mental space.

Ideally, the word "planning" should be banned from the retreat since it nudges people into thinking incrementally and tactically, and these strategic situations require more expanded thinking.

Another reason to have the leadership team do this work (at least initially) is that more junior team members may not have the external perspective or sense of empowerment to think outside of existing structures. In my experience, even when a leader asks a group of employees to think "outside of the box" and to be bold, there's often a dynamic where ambitious ideas are cut down or self-censored (e.g., "They'll never go for that." "That's interesting, but we can't prove it.").

However, like with the tiger team approach, this approach does not have to be secret or yield a binding solution. The work after the retreat will likely include getting feedback and bringing in relevant experts to test the emerging ideas.

The Leadership, Routines, and Culture Approach

If your organization faces the **Working Here Isn't Great, Stuck in Neutral,** or **Out of Control** strategy situations, the solution may not be a strategy process. These are indeed strategic issues, but a strategic planning process is likely to conclude with platitudes like, "We need to improve the culture" or . "We need more focus," which are likely already known by everyone.

Moreover, organizations often conduct time-consuming employee surveys during strategic planning that ask everyone about their experience. And when the data returns, it usually confirms what everyone already believes to be the case. Hence, the survey is not always the most effective use of resources.

The challenges in these strategic situations are likely solved by improving routines and changing the culture. Putting challenges like these into a strategy process can undermine the solution by orienting people toward creating a plan for future action. Instead, it's more powerful for leaders to start working and leading differently *right now.*

Implementing a process can also lull the team into waiting until the end of the process to take action rather than starting immediately.

The **We're Misaligned** situation presents unique challenges, but misalignment among departments or units on the strategy is also best addressed with leadership moves or improved routines.

Organizational misalignment is often caused when:

- The forums in which departments could communicate their activities and reconcile conflicts are nonexistent or do not function well
- There are interpersonal challenges between leaders that prevent them from effectively working together
- Organizational processes (e.g., performance management, compensation, role selection) create incentives for leaders to focus on what's best just for themselves or their teams

Addressing those impediments to alignment is best done outside of strategic planning processes. This is especially true because the presence of conflict or competition between leaders can turn the strategy process into yet another forum for that competition rather than a forum to achieve alignment.

Consider Skipping Strategic Planning Altogether

All the strategic situations discussed above imply a specific strategic challenge to solve or an opportunity to pursue. The remaining situations do not, so a formal strategic planning process may not be helpful.

Situation: It's All Good: If this is indeed the situation for your organization, congrats! Rather than taking on a strategy process that consumes time and energy, your organization may be better positioned to focus on tactical challenges and continuous improvement.

Situation: Time-Based Need to Plan: Nonprofits often start thinking about strategic planning once their existing plan is coming to an end. This is the worst reason to do so.

If this is where the team's analysis of your strategic situation landed, it is worth doing more work to determine what other strategic situations apply. Strategy work is more productive if everyone understands the organization's specific challenges and opportunities.

Situation: Funder-Driven Need to Plan: If creating a strategic plan is the final piece of convincing a funder to write a big check, that is undoubtedly worth the effort. However, if this is truly the *only* reason to do strategic planning, that fact should be clear to everyone. Otherwise, there is a risk that people will put excessive effort into creating a "strategic plan" when the real need is for a "marketing brochure" for the existing and already effective strategy.

ENGAGE YOUR TEAM AND TAKE ACTION!

Action #1: Pause for Alignment

Before moving forward, I strongly advise getting stakeholders on the same page with their understanding of the strategic situation. The time and effort will be well spent.

The conversations you have to generate that alignment will make the planning process smoother and can model the kind of inclusive ongoing strategy conversation that will fuel the organization going forward.

Action #2: Push for Clarity on the Strategic Issues and Turn Them into Success Criteria

In *Strategic Planning for Public and Nonprofit Organizations*, John Bryson argues that a good description of issues "(1) phrases the issue as a question the organization can do something about and that has more than one answer, (2) discusses the confluence of factors ... that make the issue strategic, and (3) articulates the consequences of not addressing the issue."[1]

Getting crisp on the strategic opportunities and issues can be useful because it allows the team to prioritize the ones that matter most. Otherwise, there can be a temptation to say, "All of this matters," leading to a bloated strategy.

Clarity on the strategic issues and opportunities also serves as a powerful tool to evaluate emerging priorities and ensure that each serves a strategic purpose and that they collectively achieve the desired impact. In the simplest terms, that would read, "Our strategy must address X, Y, and Z. If we cannot confidently say that, our work is not done."

Action #3: Identify Initiatives to Pull Out of the Planning Process

These are no-regrets activities for which no more "planning" is needed. For example, if you identified that the organization needs a process to regularly engage stakeholders, identify who can lead that process—and just do it.

Action #4: Identify (and Launch) Tests

If you identified potential strategic concepts, push to identify real-world tests that would give you meaningful data to compare them. Think: *What experiments should we start now to have good enough data to decide at the end of the process?*

By starting now, you can get a few months' worth of data to support choosing between those ideas. Conversely, if the ideas remain untested, it would be much harder to discern which is best. It's also much more likely that the debate will be resolved by picking a winner and a loser, which contradicts the overall goal of bringing the team to alignment.

GUT CHECK: DO WE HAVE THE ISSUES NAILED?

It is my experience that identifying the organization's strategic situation usually surfaces most of the important opportunities and challenges—even without doing more structured analyses like Strengths, Weaknesses, Opportunities, and Threats (SWOT) or an environmental scan. If that's the case, this provides an opportunity to speed up the process.

One way of testing whether the team has a good handle on the strategic issues is to ask, "On a scale of 0 percent to 100 percent, how confident are you that we've identified the most important issues?" People should write down their answers privately so that they are not influenced by others. The results are the first gut check about whether you are ready to move forward.

It is also worth testing the proposed list of priority opportunities and challenges with a few others who were not part of the initial discussion. Before showing those individuals the list, first ask them to state what they believe is the most important opportunity or challenge.

Then, when asking them to review the list, don't just ask for their agreement or disagreement. Instead, ask them to bring a different lens since the exercise is a test of whether the team's thought process was robust. You want questions like these:

1   What is missing?
2   What blindspots are there?
3   What stakeholders would disagree with this list?

Once you have reasonable confidence that issues reflect reality, you're ready to move forward.

KEY TAKEAWAYS

1   Before doing anything, ask yourself: *Why are we doing strategic planning?*
2   Determining your organization's strategic situation is step one in creating a planning process that addresses the most critical opportunities and challenges and includes the right people at the right time. Without that definition, you increase the odds of wasting time and effort on activities that do not matter.
3   The BIG PROCESS approach to strategy is most applicable when there is a need for substantial change and time to prepare the organization for that change. It may also be relevant when the process must appear to be robust and deliberate.
4   If the strategic challenge is clear and readily accepted, consider a tiger team of experts to solve the challenge directly.
5   If the strategic challenge requires a fundamentally new economic or operational model for the organization, you'll likely need leaders to take on this work themselves.

6   When the challenge is about the culture of the organization, you may not need a strategy process to address it. Instead, the work may be improving leadership or routines outside of the strategy process.

7   If you cannot identify a specific strategic opportunity or challenge to address, consider skipping planning altogether.

WHAT'S NEXT

Now that you've identified your organization's needs, the following chapters will help you design the planning process to meet those needs. We'll start with creating the conditions for success.

Note

1   John Bryson, *Strategic Planning for Public and Nonprofit Organizations: A Guide to Strengthening and Sustaining Organizational Achievement* (5th Ed.) (Hoboken, NJ: Wiley, 2017), 195, e-book.

References

John Bryson, *Strategic Planning for Public and Nonprofit Organizations: A Guide to Strengthening and Sustaining Organizational Achievement* (5th Ed.) (Hoboken, NJ: Wiley, 2017), 195, e-book.

Chapter 3

Creating the Conditions for Success

"I want someone to come in and shake the board and the senior leadership—really shake them up. We're nowhere near ready to start talking about strategy."

That's what the CEO—I'll call her Erica—of a nonprofit that runs study abroad programs told me about her approach to the period before her organization's strategic planning. While the organization successfully adapted its approach during the COVID-19 pandemic, the pandemic created longer-term changes in the desire and capacity for families and schools to host students. Put another way, fundamental assumptions about the programs and their impact were shifting.

That's why Erica thought the board and staff needed a shakeup. If they went directly into strategic planning with the assumptions from the past, they might not reach the right conclusions. So, instead of jumping straight into the process, Erica decided to first prime the organization for success.

To succeed in strategic planning, you should also prime your organization for the process.

The first step in priming the organization for success is to help people understand why you're taking on the effort and what it should achieve. But this work does not stop once you start crafting the strategy—i.e., conducting analysis, identifying strategic priorities, and identifying initiatives. The entire process should be inclusive, with robust communication with the rest of the organization about the emerging strategy logic.

Finally, action on the strategy should start as soon as possible. This includes both no-regrets initiatives and the work to build strategic organizational routines. Once you start acting on the strategy, you can inform it and iterate upon it with real data, not just conjecture.

However, this runs counter to how most people think about "planning"—that there is a long period of thinking and considered decision-making before implementation. Their mental model looks like Figure 3.1.

Craft the Strategy   ⟶   Implement

Figure 3.1 A Traditional Planning Process

DOI: 10.4324/9781003499619-5

To create a different expectation—that you will start taking action while crafting the strategy rather than waiting until the end—you need to articulate a different approach. If done right, your planning process should look more like Figure 3.2.

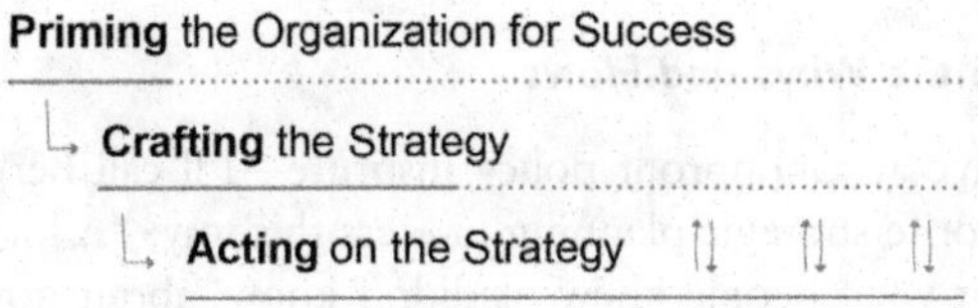

Priming the Organization for Success

⌙ **Crafting** the Strategy

⌙ **Acting** on the Strategy   ⇃↾   ⇃↾   ⇃↾

Figure 3.2 Planning with Priming and an Action-Orientation

SETTING EXPECTATIONS FOR STRATEGIC PLANNING

The terms *strategic planning* and *strategic plan* come with connotations about how people will be involved and what the final product is. Your role as a leader is to shape people's expectations of what you hope to accomplish.

Here are some principles for properly setting expectations.

1 Clarify for Yourself What the Process Is About

In the previous chapter, by articulating your organization's strategic situation, you will have taken the first step in defining what the organization needs to accomplish with planning.

Now is the time to take that analysis further by completing this sentence: "We'll be successful with strategic planning if…"

Your answer might include things like:

- Content goals—e.g., "… we answer these questions: _____.", "… we build these tools and documents: _____."
- Process goals—e.g., "… we complete the process in ___ months."
- Participation goals—e.g., "… people feel _____ at the end of the planning process."
- "Use" goals—e.g., "… we use the new strategy to _____."

This step is essential to you as a leader because you must communicate these items to help others participate effectively.

Moreover, you should articulate what topics are *in bounds* and, just as importantly, what topics are *out of bounds* for the strategy process. Part of this is helping those working on strategy know the degrees of freedom for the effort. But part of it is also just good process management.

Advancing Real Change (ARC) is a Baltimore-based nonprofit that works to make the criminal legal system more just. Erin Fiaschetti, ARC's director of operations and leader of the strategic planning process, had this advice for leaders starting strategic planning: "Make sure that they understand how open they are to change... . If things are off the table, don't set yourself up to get feedback that those are the things people want to change."

2 Communicate the Whys and Hows

A senior executive at a nonprofit policy institute—I'll call her Grace—described her least favorite strategic planning process this way: "A lot of assumptions were made about what people knew or didn't know, about how much people understood why they were doing this, and about what we were supposed to get out of it." That strategic planning process fell apart because there was no clarity about those assumptions.

As a result of that experience, as Grace prepared to lead a fundraising strategy effort, communicating the Whys and Hows to all the stakeholders was the first piece of business. She told me her approach would be, "Let's start with why we're all in this room. And let's talk about what our roles are and what perspectives I think you bring. Then we can talk about whether that's right (or not) before we even get into the meat of whatever we're supposedly discussing."

She continued, "'Strategic Plan' has connotations and comes with lots of built-in assumptions... . And if leadership is not clear about what they expect to get out of this, what [others'] role is in providing input, and how that input will be used, it gets messy right out of the gate."

I asked Anne Marie Burgoyne, the Managing Director of Philanthropy at Emerson Collective, about her insights on strategic planning success, given how many nonprofits she has supported and funded to do this work. Her first thought was also the importance of clarifying the Why.

But she added to this a second dimension: *Why is this the right time?*

In her experience, many organizations start planning with key board members and staff on different pages about whether now is the ideal moment to invest time and effort in strategic planning. She said it is easy for some people to be excited about the possibilities—e.g., the opportunity to raise money with a new plan or implement a new vision. But Burgoyne told me, "On some level, everyone has to believe it's the right time."

The good news is that starting a conversation about the right time is a great way to bring out everyone's perspectives on the organization, on the challenges and opportunities it faces, and on the urgency required to address them. And that conversation is a crucial step in building a foundation for an effective strategic planning process.

3 Don't Just Tell. Ask, "What Does 'Strategic Planning' Mean to You?"

Roshni Jain was a San Francisco Shakespeare Festival board member when the organization pursued strategic planning. Reflecting on that experience, she highlighted that board members' diverse professional backgrounds made the process more difficult. She told me, "There was definitely variation among board members on what they thought [strategic planning] means and how it works." This dynamic was exacerbated because the organization's staff were artists for whom strategic planning was "very foreign."

Spencer Smith experienced this same dynamic when he was a board member of Camp Nor'wester in Washington state. When I asked for his advice to leaders taking on strategic planning, he advised directly engaging the variation in perspectives among the board and staff by asking, "What does 'strategic planning' mean to you?"

Doing so creates an opportunity both to articulate the goals of the process on *their* terms and to clarify the Whys. In this way, it also makes setting expectations for strategic planning a two-way conversation.

Finally, you will discover that people have different working definitions for many of the other words you would use during the process—e.g., mission, vision, goal, priority, objective, and strategy. You should expect to ask, "What does that mean to you?" and to drive alignment at every step of the process.

4 Give the Process a Name That Indicates What You Want to Achieve—and No More

Changing the mission or vision of an organization is akin to amending the constitution for a country. Creating a strategic plan can feel like passing a complicated piece of legislation. Once you say you are starting those efforts, the expectations go way up for how extensive the engagement process needs to be. They become very political, very quickly.

If the goals for your strategy process are more modest, you want to do everything possible to lower these expectations. And that starts with the name of the project.

For example, if the "strategic plan" is meant to outline the major goals for the next year or so, consider calling it "Annual Goal Setting" or "Near-Term Priorities." People on the board and staff will be interested in contributing their ideas. Still, they are far less likely to see those as planning efforts that should take months to finish or to see the final product as something they should have a right to line edit before completion. These are much more like executive orders than constitutional amendments, which makes your job leading the process much easier.

Similarly, I once worked with the head of a school who called their process a "Strategy Step Back and Look Forward." Note that there is not even an implication that there will be a final "plan" document in that framing. That was good enough as long as he communicated to stakeholders what the results were.

Juma Ventures, a San Francisco-based social enterprise that operates businesses for the purpose of employing young people, provides a great example of intentional framing of a strategy effort. As Juma leaders worked on strategy with a consultant, they framed their plan as a "strategic learning agenda." Juma's CEO, Adriane Armstrong, told me, "It's not a static strategic plan. It's a plan for what we need to build in order to learn what we need to maximize impact."

This framing set the stage for an inherently dynamic approach because it constantly calls the team back to the core strategic questions rather than just the initiatives they identified at one moment in time. Moreover, the plan called for the team to build the measurement systems needed to support the learning, putting Juma in a place to better assess its impact, make adjustments to the strategy, and communicate results to funders and external stakeholders.

The lesson: You should name your strategy process in the most descriptive way possible, with a bias toward the most narrow interpretation. Some options to spark your thinking:

- Strategy Review
- Program Strategy Refresh
- Themes for the Next 12–18 Months
- Near-Term Goals
- Human Resource Planning
- Development Strategy
- Three-Year Fundraising Priorities
- Ten-Year Capital Expenditure Plan
- Mission Statement Update (Just the Words, Not the Actual Mission)

5 Beyond the Why, Communicate the Who, What, When, and Where

Most of the leadership work in setting expectations for strategic planning is about communicating the Why. However, the communications also need to include tactical information about what the process will look and feel like for others.

Those communications should include these items:

- What questions we seek to answer
- Who will lead the process
- Who will provide input, and how much time and effort this input will take
- Who will make decisions, and in what forums (i.e., where)
- When the process will start and conclude

Building Strategic FUEL: If you want to shift the organization to be more strategic, consider the planning process the start of several ongoing activities. For example, *One of our first strategic actions will be to implement continuing efforts to collect feedback from employees, clients, and stakeholders so that we can learn and update the strategy as we go along.*

"To start off the planning and execution process on the right track, high-performing companies avoid long, drawn-out descriptions of lofty goals and instead stick to clear language describing their course of action."[1]
— Michael Mankins and Richard Steele, "Turning Great Strategy into Great Performance," *Harvard Business Review*

SUCCESS ENABLERS THROUGHOUT THE PROCESS

1 High Levels of Alignment on the Current State

Alignment on the current state usually does not happen because of something trivial: Most people do not think about the organization's strategy, how the whole system works, or what is happening in the external environment regularly. Grace, the nonprofit policy institute executive, made this point to me.

When asked to reflect on previous experiences with strategic planning, she said, "I now realize … how few people in leadership have to think across the organization." Grace then described how, in her current organization, only a handful of departments—communications, legislative affairs, and development—regularly work with people across department lines to see the big picture. Those departments are also responsible for articulating what the organization does to external parties and hearing their feedback. In other words, they're the minority of employees who meaningfully think about the strategy.

But if most people in your organization—even the leaders—aren't thinking about the strategy daily or interacting with people outside the organization, they can arrive at strategic planning with wildly different perspectives. And without a shared foundation, it's harder for a group to reason why one idea or direction is better than another.

The solution is to have an always-on effort to build a shared understanding—i.e., continuous collection of insights from employees, customers, and external stakeholders, sharing those insights widely, and collectively making sense of them.

If you are starting strategic planning now and do not have these success enablers in place, it is worth investing time and effort in the early part of the process to build as much of a common foundation as possible. Especially if the strategic situation requires urgent action, you must work with the hand you're dealt.

However, if you foresee a strategy change down the line or want to have a more strategic team, building these traits will make those aspirations easier to achieve.

Specifically, before you announce a strategic planning process, you can spend a few months gathering insights from employees and external stakeholders and share those insights in low-stakes, two-way *What does this mean for us?* conversations. This allows people to wrestle with the opportunities and challenges before the organization.

Savvy leaders will also recognize this as an opportunity to give their interpretation of what the data means, which can help shape the acceptance of strategic ideas that arise from the analysis.

Building Strategic FUEL: Removing the insight-gathering efforts from a formal planning process creates two opportunities. First, it helps position them as important *ongoing* efforts—not just something to be done for a sporadic planning process. It also lowers the temperature and enables people to engage the data and debate it on the merits rather than work to achieve a specific outcome. This helps people have authentic exchanges of ideas that build a more strategic organization.

2 The Ability to Generate a Healthy Discussion

When I interviewed leaders about their experiences with strategic planning, one thing that stood out from those conversations was how the conditions for success in the process were often established years before the official kickoff of their strategic planning.

During its recent strategic planning process, ARC, the nonprofit that works to make the criminal legal system more just, adopted an expanded mission and vision. Rather than just dealing with what happens *after* someone's committed a crime, they would also work upstream to affect the systems that would prevent crimes from happening in the first place.

This new vision would imply significant changes in whom the organization hires, how it partners with other organizations, and how it does its work. However, when the changes were proposed to the board and staff, they were readily accepted, *even before the final strategy.*

ARC's Erin Fiaschetti described why this acceptance of change was possible. She said, "We've been doing a lot of work in the past couple of years that we wouldn't have thought was part of preparing for strategic planning, but it helped people practice the skill of talking about what they want their workplace to be."

By the time the organization arrived at the start of the strategic planning process, the team had the skill and the culture to have a healthy debate about new ideas, which paid off in terms of the quality of staff engagement. Fiaschetti said, "We got people's real thoughts—not people trying to guess what we thought the right answer was... . And it was collaborative. Somebody would come up with something, and the next three comments would build on or respond to what their colleague had said... . I think that the way people built on each other's comments made it feel like a creative process for them, and not just like a feedback solicitation."

It is usually *after* leaders arrive at a strategy decision that they turn their attention to convincing their organizations that the strategy is right. ARC exemplifies how this order can flip.

3 Securing Alignment at Each Step

"When should we start writing the strategic plan?"

When I work with nonprofits, this question almost always comes up in the middle of the project.

My response is usually, "We've been writing it since the start!"

That disconnect is why I bring this up to you now. Strategic planning aims to clarify the overall strategic logic and get people on board with the strategy at each step. If you're doing that well, the strategic plan—the document—should be very similar to a collated version of all the agreements you generated.

For example, as one of the first steps of the planning process, you will have identified the strategic situation the organization is in and the challenges it must solve. That is not only the foundation for strategy; it should be the first section of the strategic plan. Tactically, write those out and put them on an internal webpage or in a Word document. This will be the first part of the strategic plan.

Then, as you complete strategic analyses, you might synthesize the insights into something like "The Five Most Important Findings for Our Strategy." As with the strategic situation, the goal is to drive a robust debate about the findings and push toward alignment.

When that happens, you have the next section of the strategic plan and can add it to the same document.

Having defined what challenges you're trying to address and the findings from strategic analyses, the strategic priorities should be a logical "therefore." Again, this is a point for robust debate and agreement.

At that point, you will have a decent sketch of the core content of the plan. If you have engaged people effectively, there should be alignment about the content and a sense among the key stakeholders that they had the opportunity to shape the strategy.

The critical point here is that each part of the strategic plan builds logically upon the previous one, which matches the logic of the planning process. Accordingly, generating alignment on the strategy at every step should also generate alignment on the plan document. If you get to the end of the process, and people are reading the strategy for the first time, it's a sign that the process broke down along the way.

4 Separating Strategy Development from Strategy Writing

When you fail to separate *developing the strategy* from *writing the strategic plan* document, writing the final plan can become cumbersome and a venue for debate. That often looks like:

- Many people want to provide line edits to the plan document
- Fighting over specific wording, primarily when the disagreement is related to style and not substance

- Litigating previous agreements (e.g., "I think we need to revisit the strategic priorities.")
- Debating strategy through comments and tracked changes in a Word document rather than in conversation

To avoid this situation, you should ensure that whatever decisions are made at each step in the process are clear to everyone. That prompts them to agree (or disagree) to those decisions outside the plan document.

Creating a visual that includes "decisions we have made" and that lays out the underlying logic can also help in this effort to create the proper debates. When you engage stakeholders in the logic along the way and when they wrestle with and agree to that logic, they are less likely to wage a battle over the conclusions late in the strategic planning process.

Finally, when setting expectations about the process, you should identify the author of the plan document—i.e., who has authority over the words. Everyone else can make suggestions, but only one person should have "the pen."

KEY TAKEAWAYS

1 Most people in the organization do not regularly consider the strategy. Because of that, your role is to create a common foundation among stakeholders about what the organization faces, why it is important to do strategic planning, and why now is the right time. If you do not do this effectively upfront, there is a greater chance that people will work on the wrong things and deliver a product that does not address the most important challenges and opportunities.

2 Beyond the Why, set expectations about the Who, What, When, and Where. Providing clarity and securing agreements about roles and processes can help you avoid many of the potholes during strategic planning.

3 People have different working definitions for many of the words you might use during the process—e.g., strategy, strategic planning, mission, vision, goal, priority, objective. Don't assume you're talking about the same thing!

ENGAGE YOUR TEAM

Reflection and Discussion Questions

The main task for you—and leaders on your team—is to think ahead to potential complications in the process and identify adjustments to help prevent those complications. These questions should help you in that thinking:

1 What will be most difficult for your organization in this process?

2 What people and groups are likely most challenged by the potential strategic direction (e.g., might be negatively affected, would have to undergo significant change)?

3 What accommodations should you make in the process for those dynamics?

Download the Strategic Planning Objectives & Agreement Template

In the Bonus Resources, you will find a Strategic Planning Objectives & Agreement Template. You can use it to map your own thoughts and to capture thoughts from others on the team. The inputs will help you create a working agreement about the purpose and process of strategic planning.
www.thrivestreetadvisors.com/strategic-fuel-for-nonprofits

WHAT'S NEXT

The next chapter walks you through the final part of designing the planning process: identifying the specific people who will be involved and when.

Note

1 Michael C. Mankins and Richard Steele, "Turning Great Strategy into Great Performance," *Harvard Business Review*, July–August 2005.

References

Michael C. Mankins and Richard Steele, "Turning Great Strategy into Great Performance," *Harvard Business Review*, July–August2005.

Chapter 4

Getting the Right People Involved in the Strategy Process

If you want to get your team to invest in the strategic planning process, perhaps you should "pay" them to participate.

That's what Adriane Armstrong, the CEO of Juma Ventures, did in her organization's strategic planning effort. She realized that if the entire strategy was just "super fancy slides" developed by an external consultant, it would be harder for the team to be committed to the result. So, when talking to philanthropic funders about support for the strategic planning process, Armstrong convinced those funders to pay for the time the staff would have to spend on the process.

The leadership team was not literally paid for their time—they receive salaries, after all—but having those funds helped team members decide that strategic planning was worth their time and to invest themselves in the process. As a result of that investment, Armstrong said, "There's a level of staff comprehension and buy-in that I had not previously experienced." Not only does everyone believe in the strategy, but each leader is "viewing this three-year work plan as the number one thing they need to keep returning to every day."

Juma's experience shows just how valuable it is to get the right people involved—in the right way—in strategic planning. This chapter describes the major roles in strategic planning and how the people in these roles can best contribute. Unfortunately, there's no perfect formula for this. As a social justice nonprofit executive director told me, "You have to know your teams and know your culture." You'll read here what roles are valuable and what considerations are needed to get the most out of each participant.

As you read through each role, please jot notes about who in your organization might play the role and what it would take for them to succeed. At the end of the chapter, reflection questions help you make these choices.

> "A high-performing staff starts with putting the right people in the right places. Organizational leaders are limited to their organization's resources, but have many choices about how to use them."[1]
> "None of us is as smart as all of us."[2]
> — *The U.S. Army Leadership Field Manual*

DOI: 10.4324/9781003499619-6

ROLES IN THE STRATEGIC PLANNING PROCESS

Figure 4.1 Roles in the Strategic Planning Process

Building Strategic FUEL: The strategy process can model the inclusive and robust conversation you want to continue during implementation. At every step, you'll want to think about how to keep key stakeholders involved and signal to them that the strategy conversation will be ongoing.

THE TOP LEADER

It's probably obvious, but the organization's CEO has a significant role in strategic planning.

As described in the previous chapter, the first role of the top leader is to articulate why the organization is doing strategic planning and what it hopes to accomplish. Without that context, it is easy for people in the organization to form their own ideas about the process.

The top leader is also the most important convener of others, and especially of other senior leaders. For example, the top leader may have to clarify to other senior leaders that devoting time and attention to strategy *is* their job, not a deviation from their "real" jobs. Their felt ownership over the development of strategy is an essential enabler of effective implementation.

Beyond setting expectations, the top leaders can help shape the process's success by stating upfront their hypotheses and what constraints exist.

However, stating hypotheses and constraints does not mean leaders should share "the answer" on strategy. Doing so can get in the way of others sharing their ideas. In her book *Teaming*, Amy Edmondson advises, "When people in power speak authoritatively and speak first, it often results in greater self-censorship by others, even if this was not the original intention."[3] This also means that when the top leader is present, they may have to be quiet at the right moments to give others space to reason through strategic logic.

Finally, this expectation-setting may include articulating what constraints do *not* exist. When thinking about strategy, most people in the organization unconsciously assume the mission, core programs, and organizational structure will be the same in the future. And even if they sense that there should be change, it is hard for junior team members to call out uncomfortable truths or propose changes that might negatively impact those more senior to them.

So, when bold change is needed, the top leader must give specific permission for bold ideas to exist. And they need to encourage bold ideas to be developed without judgments that might prematurely eliminate promising ideas before they are fully developed. That might sound like:

We need at least two ideas that seem crazy.

What would we do if we were starting from scratch and could only do one program?

Instead of identifying why these ideas might not work, let's identify what must be true to make them work.

Tactically, the top leader's role may also include:

- Helping to identify people who should be engaged in the strategy process and ensuring that they can free up time to do so
- Regularly meeting with the planning lead to help resolve impediments
- Managing the board of directors' role in the strategy process
- Leading engagement with particularly important external stakeholders

THE PLANNING LEAD

Every strategic planning effort needs a lead. Even if you have a strategy working group, it is helpful to have one person who is first among equals.

The ideal person to be planning lead:

- Is a leader
- Has the ear of senior leaders
- Will be involved in implementing strategy on an ongoing basis
- Can devote at least fifteen to twenty hours a week to the planning effort

What Good Looks Like for the Planning Lead

Here are four critical roles for the planning lead. Because these are leadership roles, an insider needs to take them on. The strategy consultant can help facilitate the planning process, but they cannot serve these functions. If there is no internal leader who can play this role, it can have a significant negative impact on the planning process.

1 Making meaning

Strategic analysis does not usually yield a clear, unassailable conclusion. In the process, someone must help steer stakeholders toward what the data means.

2 Stitching strategic ideas together, with a strong editorial lens

You'll encounter multiple perspectives on the strategy. The answer is not to try putting all the ideas in one big pot. (It's not a minestrone.) Instead, the planning lead should actively reconcile the various ideas into a coherent whole, including leaving some ideas out. You want someone comfortable playing that role.

3 Actively leading

Processes fall apart if the lead only minds the "process" elements—for example, scheduling meetings. It would be best to have someone actively shaping the work and others' perspectives.

4 Setting up successful implementation by bringing in the right people at the right time

Strategic plans often falter when they are "handed" to subordinate leaders for action. Instead, the lead should bring people in as soon as needed. This helps others access the necessary context to shape initiatives and effectively take ownership.

THE STRATEGY WORKING GROUP

It's probably worth sharing a bias I have: I *hate* committees. I hate them even more when they are used in planning processes.

As my wife would attest, nothing frustrates me more than a group decision-making process. When I'm at a group dinner and it comes time to decide on the order, I'm a "just let one person decide" kind of guy. I stay silent.

My personal bias aside, there are situations in which committees can be used effectively. In the book *In Search of Excellence*, Thomas Peters and Robert Waterman profile how excellent companies leverage committees. They write:

"Yes, they too have task forces, for example. But one is more apt to see a swarm of task forces that last five days, have a few members, and result in line operators doing something differently rather than the thirty-five-person task force that lasts eighteen months and produces a 500-page report."[4]

The committees I encounter in strategic planning efforts run the gamut from smaller, productive task forces to stifling thirty-five-person affairs. Reflecting on these, the differences mainly arise from the different contexts in which they are formed.

Some observations from that experience:

1 "Representative" committees tend to slide into self-interests

I often see Noah's Ark committees in organizations—two from each department.

This is reasonable when there are legitimate reasons why departments have different perspectives. For example, left to their own devices, marketing professionals might approach a problem differently than risk management professionals. This happens because those two groups have different frameworks and approaches to guide their work.

In this case, creating formal structures to bridge their work makes sense. They can find a better answer together than apart.

However, when these committees are less about different, legitimate approaches and more about the individuals representing the interests of their respective departments, that is a problem. It assumes that each unit has a different objective function than the organization as a whole, and it increases the odds that the committee becomes about fighting for interests that are in conflict rather than a joint effort to find the best solutions.

I've seen this dynamic arise when the organization works in a siloed or overly hierarchical way. People feel they must fight for a seat at the table, owing to a lack of appropriate information sharing and collaboration. In these situations, committees are unlikely to work well because the organization doesn't work well.

2 Attempts to use committees to "build trust" in a process or decision often fail

Part of the reason leaders create Noah's Ark committees is a desire to build trust in a process or decision.

There's nothing wrong with this instinct. Many organizations are run through structures like executive committees, coordinating committees, and the like.

Where it works best, committees deliver a legitimate voice to people, and there's a foundation of trust.

Committees go wrong when they try to solve for distrust in the organization. The problem with this approach is that it rarely delivers.

If they do not believe their voice is being heard today, the average person in, say, the IT department will not be convinced that a process is legitimate just because someone from their department (whom they might not ever talk to) was present at some meeting.

The work to build an inclusive culture is essential, but a committee will not necessarily solve it. The day-to-day actions of leaders matter more.

3 Committee decision-making processes avoid conflict—and that isn't good

If you have ever participated in a group, you know it is hard for them to make decisions! In strategy processes, I've seen this manifest in several ways.

Suppose the group is too oriented toward consensus. In that case, they can sand off the most compelling aspects of potential strategies or recommend "a little of this, a little of that" solutions that are strategically incoherent.

Moreover, if the group includes junior leaders, they can shy away from solutions that require change by those above them. It is hard for them to say, "The problem is that the leadership team sucks, and we'll never make progress if they don't improve."

What are better approaches?

I Instead of a "committee," use a term like "working group," "task force," or "tiger team."

The change in semantics is part of creating a more action-oriented approach to the group.

As part of creating the group, clarify the specific deliverable, timeline, and who has decision rights. For example: Is the group submitting their ideas to the decision maker, or do they have the right to decide themselves?

2 Form the group with only those who are critical to success.

If the committee's purpose is primarily political (rather than to solve critical issues), having equal and broad representation is ideal. A Noah's Ark approach works.

In every other situation, form a group with only those with the *right knowledge* to address the issue—and no more. That is, invite someone from Finance not because Finance needs to be represented but because you want someone who *understands finance.*

Then, instruct the chosen team members to work inclusively—e.g., share updates widely, request feedback from all audiences, and pull in new people to the group when necessary. This approach is more likely to deliver on the action orientation while enabling others to feel they could contribute to the solution.

3 Help the group avoid watered-down solutions.

Here, leaders can play a role in helping a group avoid sanding down the interesting edges of their proposal by doing things like:

- Explicitly asking for bold suggestions
- Structuring the request (for instance, "I'd like you to provide one reasonable idea, one 'if we only have two days to implement' idea, and one 'if there were no constraints' idea.")
- Helping the group understand what existing constraints they should challenge

Bonus Resources

In the Bonus Resources, you can find additional guidance on what an effective working group should do, ideal profiles of its members, and how to help these groups be effective.

www.thrivestreetadvisors.com/strategic-fuel-for-nonprofits

THE LEADERSHIP TEAM

The overall leadership team has a significant role to play in the planning process.

Most importantly, they should be involved upfront to help identify the organization's strategic situation and align on the planning approach. This increases the odds that the group will embrace the final result of the process.

Along the way, the leadership team should be engaged in identifying what no-regrets actions the organization needs to take immediately. The leadership team may also focus on building more effective strategy routines (such as redesigning their meetings to be more strategic). Again, this work should happen in parallel to building the strategy.

In terms of developing the strategy, the leadership team may also support the process by:

- Completing an organizational effectiveness diagnostic
- Encouraging their teams to complete an employee experience survey to maximize response

- Providing inputs on specific strategic questions when the strategy working group brings them to the leadership team
- Sharing the emerging strategic direction with their teams and soliciting feedback

INITIATIVE AND CULTURE CHAMPIONS

As the plan comes to a higher resolution—after identifying strategic priorities—there will likely be a need to include a wider group of employees in fleshing out the strategy. Two champion roles to consider:

Initiative Champions and Owners

These leaders (sometimes junior leaders) will shape and lead specific strategic initiatives. Ideally, you'll bring these people into the process as soon as they are relevant.

They will collaborate with the planning lead and other senior leaders to shape strategic initiatives. But because they will do the work, they have the right to propose how it gets done and what tradeoffs they might have to make with existing work to do so.

Culture Champions

These are senior and junior people who will provide energy and focus on the changes the organization seeks. This is especially true where there needs to be a culture change.

For example, one organization formed an "Employee Engagement Team" whose mandate was to:

- Regularly solicit ideas to improve employee engagement from around the organization
- Find and highlight examples of people making a positive impact
- Be the beacons in their departments for improving employee engagement
- Meet with the CEO and provide "ears to the ground" feedback

Another organization considered a "Process Champions Working Group" whose mandate was to:

- Solicit ideas for improving or eliminating organizational processes
- Fill a regular slot in the leadership team meeting to raise improvement ideas so that they did not get buried
- Become experts at facilitating process redesign sessions to build capacity for doing the work in an agile way

In both cases, these champions did not have much formal power or responsibility for the initiatives. Instead, they were passionate about the work and rewarded by impact and recognition.

THE BOARD OF DIRECTORS

Determining what role the organization's board of directors should play is tricky.

The first thing to consider is that your board meetings will be more strategic, once the organization develops high-quality strategy routines. This will happen because senior leaders will have a clearer definition of success, a consistent set of quantitative and qualitative data to assess the current situations, and synthesized perspectives on what's happening in the organization.

But if your board has not been engaged in high-quality strategy discussions to date—i.e., they are not fully aware of the challenges and opportunities— here are some perspectives to help you figure out the right way to engage them in the strategic planning process:

I Align with the board on how it wants to be involved

Some boards consider setting strategy as *their* work and will want to drive it. Other boards lean on the staff to make a recommendation and only weigh in at the end. The first step is understanding how the board thinks about its ideal involvement.

2 Avoid putting board members on a strategic planning committee just because they are board members

However, if specific board members have relevant skills and are willing to be working group members, they can add substantial value.

3 Keep the entire board in the loop with the emerging thinking

For example, you want to show the steps in the logic and solicit feedback so that everyone can understand and buy into the solution when the strategy is ready for board action.

4 Do not tempt or make it easy for the board to pontificate about the strategy

A big thrust of this work is to have data and logic inform the strategy process. Hence, when you bring the board in, you'll want them to react to prompts like, "Which of these assumptions seem most valid?" Or, "How robust is the logic?" And you'll want to avoid prompts like, "What do you think we should do?"

THE STRATEGY CONSULTANT

You may have noticed in previous sections that each strategic planning approach requires a lot of effort from leaders in your organization.

Yes, it does—quite intentionally. This approach to planning aims to build the skills *inside* the organization. So, while the strategy consultant should provide excellent process management and expertise, everyone must get their hands dirty.

Beyond the planning process, leaders should get used to higher and more sustained engagement in strategy routines. This is what happens in the most effective organizations. This investment of time will provide great focus and alignment (thus saving time dealing with the effects of diffuse focus and misalignment), but it should start now.

New and prospective clients also sometimes give the following responses to this approach:

> *"That sounds good, but won't stakeholders and employees want to share feedback anonymously?"*

You should ideally hear directly from employees rather than having their feedback mediated by the consultant. Employees sometimes fear speaking up, but the right long-term solution is to start opening up conversation channels. Having the consultant drive an anonymous feedback process only punts the issue to the future.

Similarly, if the external stakeholders are important to the organization, you should hear their feedback directly. And if you think they will not be candid with you, building the kind of relationship that will make them willing to share honest feedback can start now.

In my experience, the fear that external stakeholders will shy away from direct feedback is usually overhyped. When you break the ice—"We know we're not good at X" or "We are trying to figure out how we can get better at Y"—people are generally open to providing advice, even if it includes negative feedback.

Another strategy is to ask for "feedforward" rather than feedback. Marshall Goldsmith describes it this way: "Feedforward ... is feedback going in the opposite direction. That is, if feedback, both positive and negative, reports on how you functioned in the past, then feedforward comes in the form of ideas that you can put into practice in the future."[5]

Practically, he suggests: "Ask that person for two suggestions for the future that might help you achieve a positive change in your selected behavior."[6]

With these approaches, you can get the best of both worlds—honest input on the most important topics and a way to build relationships directly:

> *"That sounds good, but isn't the strategy consultant the expert at doing those interviews?"*

I have often seen consultants overhype the value of "professional facilitation."

The problem with that view is that consultants often don't know enough to ask the right questions! Without the deep context of your organization, it is hard for the consultant to know whether what they hear in interviews is interesting.

I observed this firsthand when I was a business leader. We would use external providers for customer empathy interviews. Those professionals knew how to ask open-ended questions—something anyone can learn to do well—but they would always miss the most interesting opportunities to deviate from the interview script because they did not know the nuances of how the business or product worked.

But you, strategic leader, do have that knowledge. The strategy consultant can help prepare you for customer and stakeholder interactions and assist, but they cannot replace your expertise:

> *"That sounds good, but isn't the strategy consultant the expert at strategy analysis?"*

Yes, if your strategy consultant is good, they likely have analytical skills. But let me temper your expectations: They are probably not doing anything fancier than the analysts you have on staff. The real value in the strategy consultant is knowing what to ask (e.g., design of a survey) and what to look for.

The whole goal is to build these skills in your organization. If the strategy consultant is solving the problem *for* you rather than helping the team solve the problem for itself, it undermines long-term success. That is why you want strategic planning to be a co-learning process, and it is why you want to have an internal staff member paired with the strategy consultant at each step.

KEY TAKEAWAYS

1   By engaging the right people at the right time in strategic planning, you can start to model the ongoing and inclusive nature of the strategy routines going forward.

2   The first role of the top leader is to articulate why the organization is doing strategic planning and what it hopes to accomplish. Beyond that, she will need to provide process sponsorship to keep the process on the right track.

3   Because success in the planning process requires adept organizational navigation, every process should have an internal planning lead. It is hard for a consultant to play this leadership role.

4   Strategic planning committees are not great at creating clear strategies. Consider a smaller group, formed with only those who are critical to success. For all stakeholders in the process, including the board, role clarity creates smoother interactions.

ENGAGE YOUR TEAM

Reflection and Discussion Questions

These questions will help you and the team finalize choices for whom to involve in the planning process:

1 Who in our organization should play which role in our process?
2 What skills and knowledge are essential in the working group?
3 For the planning lead and strategy working group, what adjustments do we need to make in their current workload so that they can focus appropriately on the strategy?
4 What's our plan for engaging the entire organization authentically?
5 What will likely be most difficult for us as an organization? What can we do to avoid those challenges?

Download the Tools

In the Bonus Resources, you will find a template to note who should play each role and outline expectations for leaders' involvement in the strategic planning process.

www.thrivestreetadvisors.com/strategic-fuel-for-nonprofits

WHAT'S NEXT

After you design the strategy process, you need to get into the work. The next chapter is about the first element of Strategic FUEL—crafting a focused strategy.

Notes

1 The Center For Army Leadership, *The U.S. Army Leadership Field Manual* (New York: McGraw-Hill, 2004), 142.
2 Ibid, 141.
3 Amy Edmondson, *Teaming: How Organizations Learn, Innovate, and Compete in the Knowledge Economy* (San Francisco, CA: Jossey-Bass, 2012), 167, e-book.
4 Peters and Waterman, 120.
5 Marshall Goldsmith, *What Got You Here Won't Get You There* (New York: Hyperion, 2002), 173, e-book.
6 Ibid, 173.

References

The Center For Army Leadership, *The U.S. Army Leadership Field Manual* (New York: McGraw-Hill, 2004), 142.

Amy Edmondson, *Teaming: How Organizations Learn, Innovate, and Compete in the Knowledge Economy* (San Francisco, CA: Jossey-Bass, 2012), 167, e-book.

Marshall Goldsmith, *What Got You Here Won't Get You There* (New York: Hyperion, 2002), 173, e-book.

Thomas Peters and Robert H. Waterman, Jr, *In Pursuit of Excellence* (London: Profile Books, 1982/2015), 120.

Focused: How to Build a Strategy That Enables Impact

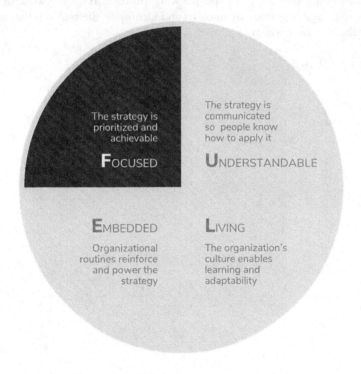

The strategy is prioritized and achievable

FOCUSED

The strategy is communicated so people know how to apply it

UNDERSTANDABLE

EMBEDDED

Organizational routines reinforce and power the strategy

LIVING

The organization's culture enables learning and adaptability

Here we are at the main event: crafting the strategy. The first step in the process of crafting strategy was identifying the current strategic situation, which you did already. The next steps all build on each other.

1   **Prioritizing and Conducting Strategic Analysis.** This will leverage the work you and the team have already done on identifying the strategic

situation. The goal is to surface the data revealing the organization's opportunities and challenges.

2   **Identifying Strategic Priorities.** These priorities should articulate the most important opportunities and challenges for the organization to take on. The critical element here is ensuring the priorities are logically based on the strategic analyses, not just a result of organizational politics. As you start to identify priorities, you may also find that you need more analysis, so the process is iterative.

3   **Identifying Strategic Initiatives.** These are the specific projects the organization will undertake to achieve the priorities. It's not enough to write down ideas and tell people to do them. To set the stage for successful implementation, the people who will have to do the work should be in charge of crafting the projects and identifying the tradeoffs they must make to achieve them.

Let's get started!

Chapter 5

Prioritizing and Conducting Strategic Analysis

IF YOU REMEMBER JUST ONE THING: STRATEGIC ANALYSIS ISN'T ABOUT FINDING THE "RIGHT" ANSWER. IT'S ABOUT SHIFTING MENTAL MODELS.

The title of this section may sound counterintuitive, so let me explain.

On one level, strategic analysis aims to get the right strategic answer. The nuance, however, is that no magic, unassailable analysis will convince everyone that the conclusions of strategic analysis are "right." This is a process filled with judgment and subjectivity.

The "right" answer is the answer that enough people believe is right and will willingly act upon

Thus, the goal of the strategic analysis phase should be to shape people's understanding of the organization, current situation, and opportunities—not just provide them with an answer.

Specifically, the ideal approach is one that:

1 Builds understanding of the external context in which the strategy is being developed
2 Exposes the logic of the strategy and invites debate about that logic rather than just giving the conclusion
3 Encourages people inside and outside the organization to reflect upon their mental models for thinking about the organization and the world around it

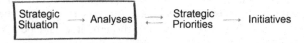

Figure 5.1 Steps 1 and 2 of Crafting the Strategy

DOI: 10.4324/9781003499619-8

Engaging with people in this way creates space for new strategies because it enables them to *reach their own conclusions* and opt in to change rather than having change thrust upon them.

As Senge writes in *The Fifth Discipline*, "The hardest lesson for many managers to face is that, ultimately, there is really nothing you can do to get another person to enroll or commit. Enrollment and commitment require freedom of choice."[1]

It's the difference between simply commanding everyone to *Run!* versus showing them the galloping tiger headed our way.

This engagement takes more time, but it saves time in the long run because more people voluntarily move in the chosen new direction and have the context to make good decisions along the way.

Data Alone Won't Necessarily Change Minds

Several years ago, I supported a nonprofit that served as a quasi-governmental regulator in developing its strategic plan. Like many organizations coming out of the COVID-19 pandemic, this client faced significant issues with employee attrition and morale, and fixing those issues was the primary focus of the strategic planning effort.

To better understand the issues, we conducted a survey of the entire staff and asked about their satisfaction, engagement, sense of psychological safety, and intent to stay at the organization. The survey results confirmed the challenges that senior leaders expected.

Only 14 percent of the staff were very satisfied working at the organization. Less than half of the staff saw themselves staying at the organization three years from then. And they reported the lowest Employee Net Promoter score that I'd ever seen—a negative 26 percent. Put another way, when asked if they would recommend working at the organization to a friend or family member, only 18 percent would strongly endorse it. More than twice that number (45 percent) would not.

We presented the survey results in a subdued Zoom meeting with the twenty-plus member leadership team. As I looked around the screen, I could see nods of agreement.

Except for one person—the leader of one of the organization's largest divisions. We'll call him David.

When we opened the floor for questions, David asked, "Well, how high should the scores be?"

I responded, "Well even if the survey indicated that 99 percent of people were satisfied, I'd still encourage you to be focused on how you can improve, since great organizations are constantly thinking about how they can get better."

David really pressed on that point. He thought it would be ridiculous to focus effort on improving employee experience if the scores were that high.

Mind you, this was two minutes (!) after discussing that the organization was *nowhere close* to 99 percent satisfaction. I also knew that David's division was usually in the middle or lower side on all of the employee experience metrics, so it was hard to understand why he was so reluctant to accept employee experience as an area for improvement.

After the meeting, I reflected on that exchange. It was a reminder that data and research are often insufficient to change people's beliefs. In this case, David stared right at the data from his own team—data stating conclusively that there was an issue—and still argued that the information was unimportant.

That's why you should not assume that quality strategic analysis will be enough to convince people of the chosen strategy. Showing more details or explaining the data one more time will not help if people do not want to listen.

Your task is to *help* them listen and find ways to shift their mental models. That's the benchmark for success in the analysis process, not just the quality of the analysis itself.

What types of analysis are likely to deliver a shift in mental models?

1 Clear Relevance

You should let the strategic situation determine the analyses that will be most informative to the most important strategy questions. This is why aligning with leaders on the strategic situation and the strategic questions that need to be answered when kicking off the process is critical.

When the team aligns on the questions, it implicitly says the answers are relevant and should motivate action.

2 Novelty

The starting place for identifying the most informative analyses is to determine what people already know or know well enough that more analysis is not helpful. My experience is that the analyses that are most likely to shift mental models are those that create novel thoughts. For example:

1   **Completely new information.** These are the areas where people would say, "We've never looked at that before," or "We haven't collected data on that in quite some time."
2   **Conflicting information.** For example, "Our customers say they want X, but they actually make decisions based on Y."
3   **Mismatches between intention and self-perception and reality.** In other words, "What we *think* is happening isn't actually happening" or, "Holy smokes, we're not as good as we think."
4   **Mismatches over time and space.** For example, "What we needed to be great at yesterday is different from what we'll need to be great at tomorrow."

Those are effective because they cause people to scrutinize their thinking, which provides a pathway for change.

Mindset shifts are less likely to happen when the analysis confirms existing beliefs. For example, if everyone believes the culture is toxic, the employee survey that shows horrendous results may not drive people to do anything about it. They might say, "That's what we expected (and have been living with to date)."

The hardest part is that the data that will cause new thinking cannot be wholly known upfront. The top leader, planning lead, and strategy consultant should discuss and determine what is likely most relevant.

Leaders must proactively help the organization absorb the strategic analysis

This advice presents a paradox: The best approach to strategic analysis is letting people develop their own reasoning toward the conclusion. At the same time, the best analyses specifically challenge their existing mental models.

At first blush, it may appear that this approach would prime people for a defensive reaction to new information while you're hoping that they come around eventually. And yes, that might be true!

So, designing the process to give people in the organization time and space to go through this evolution is critical. Some specific recommendations:

1 **Gain alignment upfront** on what strategic questions are most important.
2 **Find multiple ways to tell the data story**—e.g., anecdotes, quotes or videos of customers, quantitative analysis, and site visits. Providing various ways to consume the data is helpful because people have varying learning styles and benchmarks for "evidence."
3 **Engage on incredibly challenging information early and potentially in bite-sized pieces.** If the team discovers information that may significantly impact the organization's approach, you might tell others: "Here's what we're seeing. We want to make sure we're getting this right. What questions do you have about it? Is there something that might be causing us to misread the data? What alternative theories should we investigate?" That invitation is helpful because it creates feedback that can improve the analysis, and it causes others to reckon with the data *before* having to respond to a recommendation that might be difficult.
4 **Don't force people to face challenging data in real time.** This means providing pre-reading materials for meetings at least one to two days in advance. Ideally, you should invite others to ask questions before the meetings.

CREATING STRATEGY MAPS CAN HELP YOU KNOW WHERE TO START THE ANALYSIS

Earlier, I argued that a process that builds Strategic FUEL will invite productive debate. One place to start that debate is by creating a strategy map.

In *Making Great Strategy*, professors Jesper Sørensen and Glenn Carroll describe it this way: "A strategy map shows the arrangement of strategic concepts and resources relative to one another; it also shows the direction in which cause-like forces proceed to generate organizational outcomes. A strategy map can then be used as the basis for building the more formal logical argument needed for a rigorous assessment."[2]

Figure 5.2 shows a simplified and anonymized strategy map for one social justice nonprofit.

For this organization, creating the strategy map was useful in several ways. Historically, the organization had been focused on Mission Goal 1—making change in the current legal system. The map helped the leaders articulate that this goal was actually subordinate to the larger goal of creating more justice in society overall. That distinction helped staff and board members see why it was important to consider how it might create more fundamental changes to the legal system—Mission Goal 2.

Moreover, while the organization's strategy was complex—there were lots of initiatives happening—the map helped the team raise its gaze from the detail to how the strategy worked as a whole. This enabled much more logical thinking about where each activity fit and its purpose. For example, instead of the team

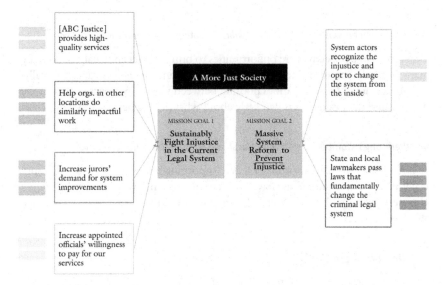

Figure 5.2 Strategy Map for a Social Justice Organization

thinking about communicating broadly about the organization's work, the strategy map helped them focus on the need to communicate with specific audiences and reason through what would cause those audiences to think differently about the criminal legal system.

Finally, the strategy map was useful in identifying what the organization *didn't* know—i.e., the logical assumptions in the map that were based on little evidence or organizational experience. These were the areas they would explore further in the strategy development process.

How to Use Strategy Maps to Inform Strategic Analysis

As an early step in the strategy analysis process, I often ask everyone on the leadership team or in the strategy working group to spend ten to fifteen minutes drawing their version of the organization's strategy. Then, we compare and discuss each other's drawings.

The exercise forces everyone to be concrete about how the pieces fit together. And because the maps are visual, they enable people to better understand others' arguments more clearly than they would through conversation. For example, at this stage, many teams will discover that they articulate the objectives differently or have different perspectives about what's most important to achieving them. This can create a foundation for the team to hash out differences in their perspectives and achieve greater alignment.

Because of that conversation, the strategy maps can inform what analyses are essential during the strategic planning process. Your team should ask the following questions:

What information would help us know which hypotheses are more likely correct?

Differences in perspectives are opportunities to bring in data and analysis. Strategy maps can help the team identify the most important places to probe. Critically, this also creates a framework for choosing between varying perspectives down the line because the discussion is had early about what people believe and why.

Are there any assumptions that are critical and that we have not tested in some time?

It is easy for an organization to leave important issues unquestioned, especially if it is successful. You may, for example, assume you know why clients choose your organization over another but not actively ask them to confirm that assumption.

Building Strategic FUEL

Why is creating a visual strategy map useful?

1   Visualizing strategy logic in a strategy map creates greater rigor by helping identify the most consequential drivers of success—e.g., where you need to put the most energy.
2   A visual map "de-egos" the debate by providing a neutral object for analysis. It enables a shift from "my idea versus your idea" to "this assumption versus that assumption."
3   A strategy map is something you can literally put on the wall, enabling it to be easily engaged going forward.
4   A strategy map helps you create a strategic dashboard by identifying what must be true for the strategy to work, supporting aligned implementation.

"As our strategic initiatives multiply, something unforeseen happens. In concentrating on all the trees, we lose sight of the forest. In a profusion of activities, an overall direction, a guiding principle, is hard to see."[3]

— Felix Oberholzer-Gee, *Better, Simpler Strategy*

THE STRATEGIC ANALYSIS YOU'LL MOST LIKELY NEED

In the following sections, you'll find an introduction to the major types of analyses to create strategic insights. They are intended to be fodder for a discussion between you, your team, and your strategy consultant on the most impactful analyses for the organization.

The major analyses are:

- Your service or product
- Employees and their experiences
- Organizational effectiveness
- What's happening outside of the organization

You'll use these analyses to determine the most important work to take on—i.e., strategic priorities. There are reflection questions at the end of this chapter, but as you read the sections, you should ask, "What is most important for us to learn?"

So that this does not turn into a dense textbook, you can find ideas about specific analyses in the Appendix.

What to Learn about Your Programs, Services, or Products

The Underlying Questions to Address

1   Is our service or product leading to the wider impact we want?
2   Who is our "ideal" client or customer—i.e., those who need or would benefit most from our service? (Note: There may be multiple "personas"

or generic descriptions of clients that fit this category. And if there isn't clarity on this question, it's worth starting here.)

3 What aspects of our product or service are most valuable to them? What aspects are least valuable? How well does our product satisfy those clients' or customers' needs?

4 In what situations do they come to us, and for what attributes of our product or service? In what situations do they go to competitors?

5 What needs are currently unmet by us? By the market as a whole?

6 How loyal are customers to us? How sticky is our product or service in their lives?

7 Where do people get stuck *before* purchasing or using our product or service? Where do people get stuck *while* using our product or service?

8 How cost-effectively are we delivering the service or product?

Why This Matters: The obvious point is that meeting your customers' and clients' most important needs is 80 percent of success in strategy.

Building Strategic FUEL: A one-time effort to understand how customers or clients value your service is helpful, but if you want to generate and sustain FUEL, you should treat the effort as the first in a regular and frequent effort to gather these insights. That practice keeps your organization relevant and enables external impact to be the judge of success.

Don't Just Measure—The Best Insights Require Talking to Real People and Seeing Things Firsthand

Do not rely on what you *think* you know or what people in the organization swear they know (but do not actively measure). In *Uncommon Service*, Harvard Business School professor Frances Frei and researcher Anne Morriss write, "A number of perfectly understandable delusions can creep into an executive's basic assumptions. A common one is overconfidence in the value you're delivering, particularly as compared with your competitors."[4]

Their research, which I agree with, is that the way to stay tethered to reality is to talk to customers directly. They write, "Don't outsource this to the marketing department. Don't consume your customers' frustration in sanitized slides delivered by direct reports with little incentive to deliver bad news. Pick up the phone, and confront the truth."[5]

But if you only have a view of the organization from second-hand data, you have false knowledge because the data that comes filtered into headquarters contains lots of bias. For example, the data often lags what is happening in the real world. Things sometimes get better or worse long before the research report gets delivered to the headquarters team.

Most egregiously, the data often reports averages when much of the actionable data happens in the extremes—e.g., fanatics who recommend you to others and haters who post negative comments on social media. I have directly worked on products where success was entirely built on whether people liked or *loved* the product. The numbers could never capture the fullness of that distinction.

Developing a nuanced understanding of the organization requires interacting with real people and products.

Or, as my friend Sandi, who runs Skilljar, a thriving customer success company, tweeted, "When in doubt, talk to your customer."[6] She added, "It requires being vulnerable to feedback and seeking contradictory points of view. But it is only through discomfort that we grow!"[7]

Watch Out: People Aren't Always Ready for the Truth

That the core product, service, or experience is of high quality is something that people in your organization might take for granted. It may be a point of pride. Very few people walk around with the belief that "we're just not that good." Because of that, it can be hard to get some to accept the need to focus on the product or service as the thing that needs to change, and there may be a belief that "We already know what clients want."

If the organization does not currently collect customer data regularly, there can be a mismatch between what everyone thinks is valuable and what customers think is valuable. That mismatch can lead to investing in the wrong parts of the product or service.

Your role as a leader may be to confront this mismatch and help bring people closer to reality.

What to Learn about Employees and Their Experiences

The Underlying Questions to Address

1 *Relative to our vision and strategy*, what cultural practices are most important to have? To what extent do those practices exist in the organization?
2 What groups of employees have the most impact on whether the organization can achieve its impact goals? How effectively is the organization delivering an experience that attracts, motivates, and retains those employees?
3 What is most important to employees' decisions about whether to join and whether to stay? How effectively do they perceive the organization as delivering on those elements?
4 How well do our job designs match the skills of employees we recruit?

Why This Matters: In most nonprofits, there's no impact without committed, quality employees. Yet few organizations take a rigorous approach to crafting a compelling employee value proposition and monitoring continually if they are delivering on it.

Building Strategic FUEL: As with the effort to collect insights from clients, you should use the strategic planning effort to develop an *ongoing* program to understand employees' experiences and the routines to act on their feedback.

Watch Out: Generic Analysis of Employee Experience

It is easy to design an employee survey that measures common aspects of culture—e.g., satisfaction, psychological safety, and engagement—without scrutinizing whether those aspects of culture are important for *your organization.* After all, the ideal norms and behaviors of the Navy SEALs are different from the ideal norms and behaviors of a nonprofit serving domestic violence victims. There's no generic "good" or "bad" organizational culture—you can only evaluate your culture and employees' experiences relative to the outcomes that are most important for your organization.

Hence, Step 1 of understanding employee experience is determining which aspects of their experience are most important for the outcomes the organization seeks. Getting alignment among senior leaders on that point is also important to enable buy-in to the implications of the analysis. In *Strategic Analytics,* Alec Levenson suggests, "In order to maximize the chances that senior leaders will act based on your analysis, you have to get alignment up front on the need for the analytics."[8]

Another driver of generic analysis is treating employees as a monolith when analyzing their experiences. In reality, different groups of employees can have significantly different experiences. For example, because feelings of psychological safety are most impacted by those you work with day-to-day, employees' ratings of psychological safety might differ across departments. Or, those employees who deliver the organization's core program and interact with clients directly might feel a higher level of connection to the mission than those in accounting or development who rarely see clients. A survey that does not recognize these potential differences will be less insightful.

Similarly, some groups of employees have a greater impact than others on whether the organization can achieve its goals. They might have specialized skills that are hard to find in the talent pool, have stakeholder relationships that would be severed if they left, or be the key points of failure in a complex system. It is worth identifying what those roles are so that you can understand their experience in greater detail.

Watch Out: Leaders May Not Be Ready for the Truth

The most challenging part of gathering employee insights is that the data usually reflects what leaders already know and experience about the culture. So, when the results confirm existing beliefs, the data may not drive new thinking that would spur action, even if the results are alarming.

Another dynamic is that leaders frequently take this data as a reflection of cultural factors outside their control rather than as a reflection *of their leadership*. Because of that, the CEO typically plays a vital role in shaping the interpretation of employee survey results and driving ownership over them.

What to Learn about Organizational Effectiveness

The Underlying Questions to Address

1 What are the *most important* tasks of the organization?
2 How effectively and efficiently is the organization doing those most important tasks?
3 What is the one thing (that we control) that holds us back from having more impact?
4 What capabilities—e.g., systems, practices, tools—are most important for achieving our go-forward strategy? Where are we strong/weak today? What do we have to build to make them strong?

Why This Matters: In most nonprofit strategic planning processes, the mission and core activities of the organization do not change. Instead, the focus is on delivering more impact with those activities, which usually requires improving organizational effectiveness.

Building Strategic FUEL: Because people in nonprofits tend to be dedicated and mission-focused, they often respond to impediments by finding workarounds that enable them to solve the problem and get back as quickly as possible to serving their clients. To build an organization with Strategic FUEL, you want to develop the organizational muscles to identify and solve their challenges systematically. That's how you can drive continual improvement and impact.

What to Learn about What's Happening Outside of the Organization

The Underlying Questions to Address

1 What are competitors doing? Why do clients, donors, and other stakeholders choose them over us—for what situations and on what attributes?
2 What trends are happening outside the organization that are affecting us today—either positively or negatively?
3 What trends will eventually affect us?

Why This Matters: Strategic shifts are often driven by external trends. Strategic planning is an opportunity to step back and think about them in a structured way.

Building Strategic FUEL: Most employees are heads-down focused on doing their job well—they do not have the time and space to monitor external trends regularly. This means that needed strategic shifts can catch them off guard. In an organization with Strategic FUEL, these employees would get bite-sized snippets of this information, putting them in a better position to make adjustments on their own (rather than forcing them to change).

Don't Just Gather External Stakeholder Perspectives. Build Relationships

The most important part of gathering stakeholder perspectives is approaching it as primarily a relationship-building effort, not just an information-gathering effort.

An important part of *ongoing* strategic success is continually gaining insights from external stakeholders about how they define success and how effectively the organization meets their needs, which is easier when they have a good relationship with the institution. With a strong relationship, external stakeholders are more likely to be candid when asked for feedback. They are also more likely to offer unsolicited feedback proactively.

If a stakeholder is important enough to hear from, they are important enough to have a relationship with. Consultants cannot do this relationship work for you.

One executive, who also served on the board of an independent school, described to me the importance of building relationships this way: "Every organization I've been in—nonprofit or for-profit—the chief executive … needs to be your Chief Sales Officer. And every time I've seen somebody abdicate that role, it hasn't gone well." It does not go well because part of showing external stakeholders that they matter to the organization is having the most senior leaders show up and solicit their thoughts directly.

Luckily, anyone can conduct a stakeholder conversation that elicits strategy-relevant information and builds relationships. These interactions are about asking open-ended questions like:

- *What criteria do you use to assess whether our organization is successful?*
- *What are we doing well, from your perspective?*
- *Where can we get better?*
- *What's happening in the market/field that you think is interesting?*
- *What will be important for our field ten years from now?*

Take Action!

You don't need a lengthy interview guide or a complicated note-taking method. Just get started!

1   Create a list of external stakeholders.
2   Identify who in the organization should lead the relationship.
3   Start scheduling calls and meetings.

4   Schedule an internal meeting for a few weeks from now to discuss what everyone is hearing.

KEY TAKEAWAYS

1   Strategic analysis is more about shifting people's mental models of the organization than simply finding the "right" answer. Doing analysis in a rigorous way is important, but the "right" answer will be a matter of subjectivity.
2   Where change is needed, engage people in the analysis in ways that provide time and space for them to wrestle with the challenges. This enables them to convince themselves and opt in to change rather than having change thrust upon them.
3   Use the strategy logic (e.g., strategy map) to decide the most useful analysis, then use the results to explicitly update the strategy logic. Those actions will help you drive a process of developing strategic initiatives—the next step—that are based on logic rather than politics.
4   Approach gathering stakeholder perspectives as a relationship-building effort, not just an information-gathering effort.
5   To fuel a dynamic strategy going forward, conduct the insights activities—e.g., understanding employees and their experiences and connecting with external stakeholders—with an eye toward making them repeatable routines.

ENGAGE YOUR TEAM

Reflection and Discussion Questions

1   What is most important for us to learn as an organization?
2   Based on my current hypotheses of our future strategy, what information would give us confidence to go in that direction? What information would disconfirm the hypotheses?
3   Based on my current hypotheses of our future strategy, what data will be most important for shifting leaders' thinking toward the direction?
4   What needed mindset shifts will be challenging for the organization? What data would help people think differently in those areas?

Notes

1 Peter Senge, *The Fifth Discipline: The Art and Practice of the Learning Organization* (New York: Crown Business, 2006), 282, e-book.
2 Jesper B. Sørensen and Glenn R. Carroll, *Making Great Strategy: Arguing for Organizational Advantage* (New York: Columbia University Press, 2021), 35.
3 Felix Oberholzer-Gee, *Better, Simpler Strategy: A Value-Based Guide to Exceptional Performance* (Boston, MA: Harvard Business Review Press, 2021), 13, e-book.

4 Frances Frei and Anne Morriss, *Uncommon Service: How to Win by Putting Customers at the Core of Your Business* (Boston, MA: Harvard Business Review Press, 2012), 42, e-book.
5 Ibid.
6 Sandi Lin, "When in doubt, talk to your customer." Twitter, January 14, 2022, https://twitter.com/sandislin/status/1482154562718818306?s=20.
7 Sandi Lin, "Yep. It requires being vulnerable to feedback and seeking contradictory points of view. But it is only through discomfort that we grow!" Twitter, January 14, 2022, https://twitter.com/sandislin/status/1482356594046214145.
8 Alec Levenson, *Strategic Analytics: Advancing Strategy Execution and Organizational Effectiveness* (Berrett-Koehler Publishers, 2015), e-book, 40.

References

Frances Frei and Anne Morriss, *Uncommon Service: How to Win by Putting Customers at the Core of Your Business* (Boston, MA: Harvard Business Review Press, 2012), 42, e-book.

Alec Levenson, *Strategic Analytics: Advancing Strategy Execution and Organizational Effectiveness* (Berrett-Koehler Publishers, 2015), e-book, 40.

Sandi Lin, "When in doubt, talk to your customer." *Twitter*, January 14, 2022, https://twitter.com/sandislin/status/1482154562718818306?s=20.

Sandi Lin, "Yep. It requires being vulnerable to feedback and seeking contradictory points of view. But it is only through discomfort that we grow!" *Twitter*, January 14, 2022, https://twitter.com/sandislin/status/1482356594046214145.

Felix Oberholzer-Gee, *Better, Simpler Strategy: A Value-Based Guide to Exceptional Performance* (Boston, MA: Harvard Business Review Press, 2021), 13, e-book.

Peter Senge, *The Fifth Discipline: The Art and Practice of the Learning Organization* (New York: Crown Business, 2006), 282, e-book.

Jesper B. Sørensen and Glenn R. Carroll, *Making Great Strategy: Arguing for Organizational Advantage* (New York: Columbia University Press, 2021), 35.

Chapter 6

Turning Analysis into a Focused Strategy

DANGER! DANGER!

You have probably put a lot of work into a robust set of strategy analyses. That's great, but you're at the trickiest part of the process—deciding what priorities to take forward. This is the heart of setting the strategy. It's also where the stakes get higher.

Choosing strategic priorities is one of the most fraught points for strategy development because people start to think about not just what the "right" answer for strategy is but also what it means *for them*. Setting priorities can mean, among other things, shifting resources from one department to another, stopping some activities to make space for new ones, or redefining what's important in the organization. And because those shifts can create perceived winners and losers, setting priorities can implicate organizational politics in ways that earlier steps in the strategy process did not.

Moreover, organizations tend to resist prioritization. So, while you are trying to make *choices* that yield a focused strategy, stakeholders often instinctively search for compromises and "all of them are important" solutions. However, the failure to make clear choices increases the likelihood that the organization will lack the capacity to take on the strategy effectively.

If your organization is like most nonprofits, everyone already has a full plate!

No magic algorithm can convert the analyses to priorities while avoiding these challenges. Instead, the conversion process requires lots of judgment and leadership. The rest of this section provides guidance to help you navigate this step.

Figure 6.1 Steps 3 and 4 of Crafting the Strategy

DOI: 10.4324/9781003499619-9

TRANSLATING ANALYSES INTO STRATEGIC PRIORITIES

Best Practices for Developing Strategic Priorities

1 Limit the number of strategic priorities.

You want *at most* three strategic priorities because greater focus enables organizations to achieve more. Tactically, the organization can only absorb so many new efforts at once, and when there are too many priorities, it is harder for people to understand the core strategic concept.

The strategy analysis phase will likely yield many areas the organization could focus on. To get to the ones that will be most impactful, I recommend asking, "What is our most important strategic challenge?" You will have discussed this in the initial leadership conversations about the organization's strategic situation.

The right strategic priorities are likely those that directly address those challenges.

Or, if the ideas that are percolating from the strategy working group do not directly address those challenges, it may be time to go back a step.

Watch Out: "Everyone should see themselves in the plan."

When people in the organization voice this sentiment, the fear is that if everyone's work is not prominently displayed in the strategic plan, some might think that their work is unimportant. This is a reasonable thought.

However, if the solution is to include everyone's work, the plan will become a laundry list of goals, which is unhelpful in signaling what matters most.

The analogy would be stating a New Year's resolution like this: "The main goal for this year is to get in shape ... but of course, I also want to do well at work, improve our finances, maintain good relationships with my family, and have fun." When stated that way, the emphasis is lost.

This is hard. (Trust me, I have lost this argument in several strategic planning processes.)

What leaders can do is clarify how the few strategic priorities relate to the ongoing goals and tactics of the organization. Namely, the latter will continue, and everyone should ask how their current work should change to support the most important strategic goals.

"Good design is as little design as possible. Less but better—because it concentrates on the essential aspects, and the products are not burdened with inessentials."[1]
— Dieter Rams, as quoted in *Dieter Rams: As Little Design as Possible*

---

2 Drive for coherence among the priorities.

Harvard Business School professor Michael Porter writes in the *Harvard Business Review* that effective strategy arises from making coherent choices that "fit" the overall strategy.

Organizations can achieve this fit by ensuring their choices are consistent. Porter writes, "Consistency ensures that the competitive advantages of activities cumulate and do not erode or cancel themselves out. It makes the strategy easier to communicate to customers, employees, and shareholders, and improves implementation through single-mindedness in the corporation."[2] A second form of fit "occurs when activities are reinforcing."[3]

The risk of not forcing clear and coherent choices in the strategy process is that it weakens the strategy.

It's like a restaurant offering five types of cuisine—it almost never works.

Watch Out: A group decision-making process that tends toward "a little of this, a little of that" or its evil twin, "all of these are important."

Leaders' first task is to push for a healthy debate that achieves greater coherence. This is why setting clear expectations for decision-making upfront is so important. Clearly stating what challenges and opportunities the strategy must address creates a more objective framework to evaluate the ideas on the table. Rather than have debates centered on "I like this idea better," the team can ask more constructive questions like, "Will accomplishing this proposed priority solve the strategy issue(s) we identified earlier?"

3 Ensure the decision process reflects strategic logic, not internal politics.

Keeping the decision process grounded in strategic logic is a challenge at every step of the process. One way to avoid this challenge is to create a visual of the strategic logic and "decisions we have made" to make it ever-present for the group. That visual can bring the group back when setting strategic priorities deviates from those early agreements.

If you create strategy maps earlier in the process, it can also help you identify strategic priorities. The first step is to update the consolidated strategy map based on the analyses you did in the process. This will mainly entail clarifying assumptions and logic. Once that process is complete, it should be apparent where the weak points are in the strategic logic. Those weak points represent areas that, if not addressed, would inhibit the organization from reaching its goals.

Most importantly, the team's earlier alignment around the strategy map creates a common foundation for identifying strategic priorities based on logic rather than politics.

Watch Out: "Do we know enough information to make a decision?"

Strategy entails uncertainty because, of course, no one knows what the future holds. But what can happen when translating strategic analyses to priorities is that uncertainty causes hesitation. When not corralled, this instinct can lead to doing more analysis ... and then doing more analysis ... and then doing even more.

There's no end when the benchmark is eliminating uncertainty.

The suggestion from A.G. Lafley and Roger Martin in *Playing to Win* is to respond to objections about an emerging strategic path with the question, *What would have to be true?*

That question can convert uncertainty to a set of premises that the group can judge as more or less critical. For the most critical assumptions, the group can then identify the additional data or analysis required to feel reasonably confident making that assumption.

Beware of Soft Agreements

One of the most challenging parts of strategic planning is the transition from articulating broad aspirations to identifying the actual priorities and initiatives that you will pursue.

On the face of it, much of this work has the tone of reaching "alignment" among senior leaders. **But as you seek alignment, first seek disagreement.**

Here's the reason: Strategic initiatives that do not compel arguments are probably not compelling.

For example, you don't need to argue if strategy does not force you to do anything differently or sacrifice anything.

You don't need to argue if an initiative is so vaguely worded that it could hold everyone's interpretation.

You don't need to argue if everyone's ideas are included in the final version, rather than prioritizing the best ones and saying *No* to the rest.

Of course, good strategy requires focus, clarity, and reinforcing activity. So, if the alignment conversation is oriented toward consensus or does not inspire robust debate, it's unlikely to lead to an effective result.

In the book *Making Great Strategy*, Sørensen and Carroll discuss how robust argument is a cultural no-no at most organizations. But, leaders' reluctance to argue the merits and logic of their chosen strategies simply delays the inevitable conflict. They give a great example of how this happens:

"[T]wo colleagues might agree that outsourcing part of the product development process is preferable to doing the work in-house—but they may each believe that for very different reasons. That may not seem to matter at first—at least they agreed and avoided a fight! But when it comes to implementation and subsequent decision-making, these unstated disagreements can be quite consequential. One person may favor outsourcing because he thinks it will be cheaper than internal development; the colleague may favor it because she thinks it will allow access to superior product development capabilities. At worst, the two will work at cross-purposes, for example, by alienating a high-quality developer through penny-pinching. At best, the fight simply got postponed."[4]

I've most often seen this manifest in organizations when leaders articulate aspirations or intentions but claim they are strategic initiatives. The giveaways are strategies that include "thinking words," like *focus on* or *be more*.

Instead, the sign of a strategy worth debating is that it contains "acting words" like *create, eliminate, invest,* and *move.*

Acting words compel debate because they require something of leaders. If you ask me to "Be more agile," my reaction is, "Sure. Sounds good." But if the request is to "Increase agility by reducing process steps and process time by 50 percent," then I've got work to do.

If the strategy is listed as "Focus on growth," it's easy to claim success. If, instead, the strategy is to "Shift at least $2M of capital expenditure from stable businesses to those with at least 40 percent growth potential by Q2," there's a set of real decisions to be made.

In the previous examples, the first kinds of strategies can generate soft agreement—i.e., a vocal yes, with an uncertain commitment to action. But, the second statements demand greater engagement and debate because they require a harder agreement. Better solutions are likely to emerge through the "hardness" of the debate.

Test: Is the Strategy Focused?

The strategic priorities represent the bulk of the strategy. But before launching into the creation of initiatives, you should go back to the prompts from earlier to test whether the emerging strategy is focused:

1 The organization has a clear mission statement.
2 The organization has a clear vision of the impact it seeks to make (e.g., offering what, to whom, for what purpose).
3 The organization has defined the critical steps to reach that vision or strategic destination.
4 The organization has identified programs or services, customer segments, and activities that fall outside of the vision and is willing to sacrifice them to focus on the most critical areas.
5 The organization has defined the most important capabilities required to reach the strategic destination.
6 The organization has identified capabilities where it is willing to be mediocre or even weak in order to concentrate attention and resources on the most important capabilities.
7 The current strategy directly addresses the most critical challenges or impediments to success.
8 The organization has an economic model that enables it to achieve its vision and be reasonably sustainable going forward.

If you can confidently answer *Yes* to those prompts, the organization is ready to start turning the priorities into initiatives.

Gut Check: Does the Strategy Really Address the Most Important Opportunities and Challenges?

The reason to identify your organization's strategic situation and get the team aligned on that assessment is that you will have identified the most important opportunities and challenges. The emerging strategic priorities should speak directly to those opportunities and challenges and equip the organization to address them.

This is a crucial test of whether the priority development process stayed true to the strategy logic or whether other factors intervened. If you cannot confidently state how each of the priorities will enable you to pursue the opportunities or tackle the challenges, it's worth spending more time on the priorities.

TURNING STRATEGIC PRIORITIES INTO INITIATIVES

Even if the strategic priorities logically follow from the most important opportunities and challenges, there is still a risk when it comes to translating the priorities into specific initiatives. This step requires the CEO and planning lead's heavy involvement. Success shouldn't be assumed.

Best Practices

1 Identify and bring in the initiative owners as soon as possible.

The best practice is that every strategic initiative must have an owner or champion—a specific human being, not the name of a department. You need to name a specific human because they will say, "Yes, I agree to be responsible for the success of this initiative." And because they are responsible, they will proactively consider the challenges, resource needs, and tradeoffs required. Committees cannot do this work effectively.

The initiative owner does *not* need to be a senior leader. The ideal owner should control most of the organizational resources and skills required to complete the initiative, even if they must bring others in to help.

When the initiative is unassigned or assigned to multiple parties, there is a risk that critical thinking about tradeoffs will not occur before the plan is final, which increases the likelihood that during implementation, you'll hear, "We don't have the resources to get that done." Or "We have too much on our plates." You want to sort those impediments out now!

Defining something as a strategic initiative implies that it's more important than some existing activities, and the plan should reflect that.

2 Empower owners to shape the initiative (but there may be negotiation).

For the initiative owner to feel ownership over the initiative, they need to have the right to shape it. As I wrote earlier, it's disrespectful if they are not given that power.

That said, there may be an active negotiation.

For example, a potential initiative owner might say, "I don't have the capacity to lead this."

The negotiation might look like responding, "I know you're slammed, but this work is important to the organization, and I'd value your leadership. Let's discuss what's on your plate and how this new work fits into those priorities. I'm open to you proposing what we'd have to STOP to make room for this new work."

Another frequent objection is that there are insufficient resources to complete the work. For example, "It would require us to hire 100 more people to accomplish this."

To these concerns, you might say, "Hiring that many people would be hard for us to do, but I hear you on the workload. We may be able to bring people in from other departments as part of our organizational focus on this effort. We also may be able to slim down other parts of your work and shift people from there."

3 Encourage and give license to the initiative owners to be bold.

Especially if the initiative owners are more junior, they may inaccurately assume organizational constraints when developing their strategic initiatives. The planning lead and the CEO can help ensure that the initiatives are sufficiently bold by:

- Clarifying what organizational constraints the strategy wants to eliminate
- Providing clarity about what the top leader is willing to do to support the effort
- Asking, "What constraint, if solved, would help you accomplish this more effectively?"
- Asking, "What do you need from senior leaders to make this happen? Please be bold and direct in your request. I can help with that."

Test: Is the Strategy "Implementation-Ready"?

You may have noticed that there is no "Create an Implementation Plan" section of this chapter on developing strategy. That is intentional.

The most critical part of implementation is fleshing out the strategic initiatives. Namely:

- Identifying the owner of the initiative—the person who will be responsible for leading the work
- The owner developing a plan for how to achieve the objectives
- The owner nominating the tradeoffs (e.g., what the organization would have to *stop* doing to make space for the new activity) or additional resources required to achieve the objectives

The critical test for leaders is to ensure that those details are sufficiently discussed and agreed to before the strategy is finalized.

Strategic plans can falter when organizations realize belatedly that the work is more challenging or resource-intensive than they thought. They can also falter if junior leaders try to add new activity to their already full plates, potentially because they do not feel free to drop any existing work.

Leaders will know that they have created an implementation-ready plan if they can say *Yes* to the following statements:

- There is a collective understanding of the tradeoffs entailed in the proposed strategy.
- We understand at a high level how to sequence activities (e.g., hiring a new Chief Development Officer before starting a campaign).
- We have done enough diligence on the go-forward economics to know the plan is reasonable.
- We know the major commitment moments in the future (e.g., deciding between two paths, having to commit significant funds) and the criteria for making decisions at those points.

High-quality implementation is also driven by creating high-quality strategy routines. That is covered in a subsequent chapter.

Gut Check: Subtraction Needed!

You cannot add an activity without subtracting some other place—unless you are the rare nonprofit that has the infinite ability to raise funds and hire new staff.

If the initiative plans do not include words like *delay, eliminate, phase out, replace, sell,* or *cancel,* there is more work to be done. Your role—and the role of other leaders—is to make clear to initiative owners that they have the license to propose those solutions.

KEY TAKEAWAYS

1   Creating strategic priorities is the trickiest part of planning because it shifts the process from one of analysis and imagination to one of tradeoffs.
2   Limit the number of strategic priorities. The fewer the strategic goals, the better. Focus enables organizations to achieve excellence. Tactically, you want only two to three strategic priorities.
3   Many organizations and teams instinctively resist prioritization and may instead search for "all of the above" or "a little of this, a little of that" solutions. However, the failure to make clear choices increases the likelihood that the organization will lack the capacity to take on the strategy effectively.

4   As you seek alignment, first seek disagreement. Strategic initiatives that do not compel arguments are probably not compelling.
5   Creating tools and visuals that get people robustly debating strategic logic and being inclusive of the doers can serve as a model for the culture of learning and adaptation that you want going forward.
6   Identify and bring in the initiative owners as soon as possible, empower them to shape the initiative and suggest tradeoffs, and give them license to be bold.

WHAT'S NEXT

In the last two chapters, we've outlined the core part of the strategic planning process. But the most important thing to remember is that it's not just *what* you do; it's *how* you do it.

At every step, making decisions explicit and securing alignment about the strategy logic helps you ensure that the emerging strategy is clear, simple, and addresses the most important opportunities and challenges.

Those steps help make strategy something everyone understands and uses to guide their work. The next chapter provides even more guidance on effectively communicating the strategy.

Notes

1   Sophie Lovell, *Dieter Rams: As Little Design as Possible* (New York: Phaidon Press, 2011), 355.
2   Michael Porter, "What is Strategy?" *Harvard Business Review*, November–December 1996. https://hbr.org/1996/11/what-is-strategy.
3   Ibid.
4   Jesper B. Sørensen and Glenn R. Carroll, *Making Great Strategy: Arguing for Organizational Advantage* (New York: Columbia University Press, 2021), 23.

References

Sophie Lovell, *Dieter Rams: As Little Design as Possible* (New York: Phaidon Press, 2011), 355.
Michael Porter, "What is Strategy?" *Harvard Business Review*, November–December1996. https://hbr.org/1996/11/what-is-strategy.
Jesper B. Sørensen and Glenn R. Carroll, *Making Great Strategy: Arguing for Organizational Advantage* (New York: Columbia University Press, 2021), 23.

Understandable: How to Communicate the Strategy So People Get It

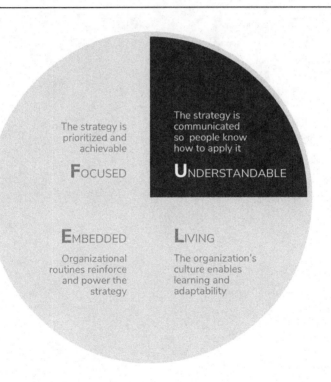

Chapter 7

Communicating Throughout the Strategic Planning Process

It's not what you say. It's how _everyone else_ hears it.

Communicating the strategy is a separate chapter here, but if you want to generate and sustain Strategic FUEL, the communication should not be a one-time—or one-way—effort. Because the process of understanding and making the strategy their own takes time, you should look for opportunities to engage people throughout the planning process.

Some of the most important opportunities include:

- **Sharing why the organization is taking on strategic planning in the first place.** This enables you to communicate what you believe is important and to invite others to share feedback.
- **Sharing findings of the strategic analysis.** This provides an opportunity to share the emerging strategy logic and allow people to wrestle with the facts.
- **Sharing results of employee surveys or focus groups.** This is related to sharing the strategy analysis, with the added benefit of signaling to employees that they are being heard and that their experience matters to the organization's overall direction. This impact is even more substantial when leaders directly engage in two-way conversations with employees about the data.
- **Including people who do the work in shaping the initiatives.** Not only does this mean sharing context for why the strategic priorities were selected, it also creates a situation in which initiative owners feel ownership over the strategy. When working with their teams, they can articulate the strategy as something they shaped rather than a burden placed upon them from above.

Strategic plans often fail to gain traction when people in the organization do not understand the strategy or think of it as an abstract concept rather than something that should affect their day-to-day work. This chapter should help you ensure the strategy is understood and real for everyone in the organization.

DOI: 10.4324/9781003499619-11

LEADERS SHOULD CREATE AUTHENTIC DIALOGUE

In many strategic planning processes, leaders and consultants believe that including staff in an employee survey is sufficient for them to share their voice and gain trust. Don't believe that.

Answering the survey never helps people feel engaged or heard. Think about the last time you completed a comment card or feedback survey in your own life. Did that make you feel like you contributed to their strategy? My guess is no.

Having a "representative" strategic planning committee does not necessarily help either because they are a drop in the bucket compared to the experiences employees have outside of the planning process. The extent to which they feel heard and believe they contribute to strategy is based on how they are included in ongoing organizational routines.

What we're going for is authentic dialogue.

What this looks and sounds like:

a   Leaders share the conversations they are a part of with their teams. For example, "In the leadership team meeting this week, we were focused on _____. Here's how I think this will affect us. What do you all think?"
b   Leaders getting feedback along the way. "The way the strategy is coming together, we're leaning toward _____. What do you all think are the implications for our team? What should I be taking back to the full group?"

Operating in that manner is novel for some leaders. If they are not doing that today, they should start! That dialogue is essential for the ongoing strategy process because that is how organizations surface new ideas and maintain focus.

USE THE PROCESS TO BUILD A SHARED VISION

In his book *The Fifth Discipline*, Peter Senge writes about the value of a shared vision: "You cannot have a learning organization without shared vision. Without a pull toward some goal which people truly want to achieve, the forces in support of the status quo can be overwhelming."[1]

A shared vision binds people to the organization because they authentically believe in it. Senge contrasts this authentic belief with selling a vision from on high:

> *"[I]t is common to hear managers talk of getting people to 'buy into' the vision. For many, I fear, this suggests a sales process, where I sell and you buy. Yet, there is a world of difference between 'selling' and 'enrolling.' 'Selling' generally means getting someone to do something that she might not do if she were in full possession of all the facts. 'Enrolling,' by contrast, literally means 'placing one's name on the roll.' Enrollment implies free choice, while 'being sold' often does not."[2]*

The strategic planning process should support building this shared vision by engaging internal stakeholders.

As mentioned in the previous section on the role of the leadership team, the place to start with employee engagement is authentic dialogue. In my experience, most employees neither want nor expect to be in on each decision. Instead, they want to feel like their voice matters. And the best way to achieve that is through the leaders they work with regularly.

An essential role of the strategy working group is to bring in people as their knowledge and perspective become relevant. This might mean asking those people questions or including them in one-time meetings. It might also mean enrolling them as a working group or task force member when their knowledge or skills best position them to work on a strategy question.

Leaders should focus on progressive disclosure. Often, leaders give strategic planning updates to the organization that focus exclusively on the process—e. g., what steps have happened already and when the process is expected to be complete. Instead, leaders should focus these updates on the *actual content* of the emerging strategy.

For example, that could be all-staff emails or communications with titles like:

- The Top Strategic Challenges We're Wrestling With
- Strategic Implications of the Employee Survey
- What Customers and External Stakeholders Are Saying About Us

Sharing the emerging strategy along the way helps the wider team better understand the context and logic behind the eventual strategy choice.

> "Communicate everything you possibly can to your [employees]. The more they know, the more they'll understand. The more they understand, the more they'll care. Once they care, there's no stopping them."[3]
> — Sam Walton, *Sam Walton: Made in America*

BEST PRACTICES FOR ENROLLING OTHERS IN THE STRATEGY AND JUMP-STARTING ACTION

If you've followed the guidance in this book, communicating the emerging strategy with internal and external stakeholders is straightforward because those stakeholders have already been in authentic dialogue with you about where the organization is headed. That means they will already understand the context within which you have chosen a strategic direction.

Still, the top leader has a significant role in formally starting the strategy implementation. Here are some best practices to guide your action.

Develop a Strategic Principle

The strategy literature argues for simple communications that are clear enough to guide people to the right actions without precise direction.

One framing for this is a strategic principle. In the *Harvard Business Review* article "Transforming Corner-Office Strategy into Frontline Action," Bain & Company consultants Orit Gadiesh and James Gilbert define the strategic principle as "a memorable and actionable phrase that distills a company's corporate strategy into its unique essence and communicates it throughout the organization."[4]

One example they give is from Walmart: "Low prices, every day." Another is from GE: "Be number one or number two in every industry in which we compete, or get out."

While the phrases are simple, they reflect complex thinking. The GE strategic principle, for example, could just as soon be written as *As a conglomerate, our only rationale for being in an industry must be having the capabilities required to be a leader of it—i.e., to be number one or number two. If not, being in the industry is not an optimal use of investment capital, and we should exit.*

But that phrasing doesn't fit on a poster.

Another way to think about the principle is what you might say at the end of a long speech on the strategy. And it would probably include a phrase like *When in doubt...* or *All else equal...* or *If you could only prioritize one thing... .*

The goal is to translate the larger goals into specific actions or mindsets that employees will take forward. This also shifts the strategy from something senior leaders do to something everyone has a role in.

A classic example of this is British Admiral Horatio Nelson's instructions to his fleet before the Battle of Trafalgar: "[I]n case Signals can neither be seen or perfectly understood, no Captain can do very wrong if he places his Ship alongside that of an Enemy."[5]

Translation: In the absence of further instruction, get aggressive.

Find a Focusing Question

A big part of the top leader's implementation role is maintaining focus on the strategy. McKinsey & Company senior partners Carolyn Dewar, Scott Keller, and Vikram Malhotra write in *CEO Excellence* that "the best CEOs invariably dwell on the elements that will make the biggest difference and encapsulate those in a pithy word or phrase that they consistently invoke."[6]

One clear forum for driving focus is in the formal routines. Indeed, the routines should be designed to ask the most important questions directly. For example, if you ask leaders in operational reviews to regularly report on what they are doing to improve employee experience, they are likely to focus on it. No one wants to look like they are slacking in front of their peers!

In *Organizational Culture and Leadership*, former MIT professor Edgar Schein describes how useful these focused communications can be. He observes, "Even casual remarks and questions that are consistently geared to a certain area can be as potent as formal control mechanisms and measurements."[7]

A helpful tactic for leaders is to translate the overall strategy into a focusing question. In *CEO Excellence*, the authors quote Sundar Pichai, CEO of Alphabet (the parent company of Google), describing how he uses this tactic to reinforce strategy themes in operational reviews. "If 'Asia Pacific–first' is one of our five themes, I could be in a YouTube review and probe the team: 'Can you tell me how you're solving for Asia Pacific first?' "[8]

Leaders can also take this approach in their wider interactions with employees. Again, from Dewar, Keller, and Malhotra:

"A less obvious but extremely powerful tool we've seen CEOs use is turning their cultural themes into questions. At Siam Cement, Kan Trakulhoon used this approach to bolster his culture of innovation. As he visited various sites, he always made it a point while on the shop floor to ask, 'What are you working on to improve your process and your productivity?' "[9]

The result? "When he came back for his next visit, however, you can bet everyone on the shop floor was ready with an impressive answer."[10]

That last part is powerful—the focusing question engaged *everyone* on the shop floor in the strategy. Like the strategic principle, this is a tool for converting the strategy from "something senior leaders are doing" to "something you, average person in the organization, are contributing to."

Be Prepared to Repeat Yourself

Sustaining attention on the strategy often requires repeating oneself.

Richard Buery, Jr., former CEO of Children's Aid Society, articulated the challenges of communicating effectively to the entire organization when you cannot reach every person directly. Buery learned "the importance of being clear and concise in your communication—not ten messages, but two or three messages repeated over and over and over again in every way you can and every opportunity you have."[11]

Drew Faust, the former president of Harvard University, described having this same experience as her leadership scope increased. "Someone would say, 'Well, you've never talked about X,' and I'd say, 'I've talked about that here, here, here. I talk about that all the time.' Then I realize that 'all the time' isn't enough. You have to do 'all the time,' and more."[12]

This "all the time, and more" communication takes discipline for leaders since it can get boring—even for you! A client of mine, the CEO of a large nonprofit, compared the repetition to a politician giving the same stump speech over a long election campaign.

However, the return from the investment in repetition is that, after hearing the same message multiple times, employees and external stakeholders are much more likely to understand the direction and their role in making the strategy a reality. When they truly get the strategy, the organization gains momentum from dozens, hundreds, or even thousands of people marching in the same direction.

Engage Beyond the Top Team

Another tool for leaders looking to ensure effective strategy is engaging more fully with those outside the senior leadership teams.

For example, *CEO Excellence* describes how Ivan Menezes, the CEO of Diageo, "makes a point to have one-on-one catchups with the top eighty people in the organization twice a year."[13]

Lynn Good of Duke Energy has a similarly intense approach. "I make a concerted effort to spend time with my direct reports, their direct reports, as well as the people who run large operations. I get them together for an hour and a half each month on strategic topics. We get together once a quarter for a longer session. We get together once a year for a day and a half."[14]

When I share these examples with clients, the first reaction is usually, "That sounds like a lot of meetings!"

I agree, but it's worth it.

Direct engagement—who you choose to meet with—is one of the few leadership tools over which you have full control. Meeting with people directly is the means by which your focusing question gets asked, for example. By engaging with a broader group of leaders—both individually and in group settings—you can avoid the game of Telephone, which can lead to your well-crafted communications about the strategy getting diluted and altered. These meetings can also be a critical check that subordinate leaders are taking the steps required to implement the strategy.

Finally, direct engagement helps you solve the political challenges of strategic change. As Dewar et al. write, "Building a broader leadership coalition not only gives CEOs more leverage in driving the organization forward, but it also puts pressure on the top team members who must respond to the leaders below them whom the CEO has trained to have the same vision about the direction of the company."[15]

ACCEPT THAT NOT EVERYONE WILL LIKE THE STRATEGY

There are a lot of definitions of strategy in the academic literature. One of the best is Harvard Business School professor Michael Porter's statement, "Strategy is making trade-offs in competing. The essence of strategy is choosing what *not* to do."[16] That is, the mark of a good strategy is that it defines objectives, scope, and activities precisely enough that what fits and *does not fit* in the strategy is clear.

This is important because it's impossible to serve every need of every customer in every geography. Investing a high level of effort, resources, and attention in every organizational activity is also typically infeasible.

What that means organizationally: Whatever strategy is set, some team members will not like it.

In fact, if everyone likes the strategy, it's probably not a good one

While the research is crystal clear on the benefits of focus and alignment, it does not articulate how leaders should deal with the organizational fallout of those decisions.

For sure, the fact that some people will not like the decision that is made—whatever it may be—is a testament to why strategic leadership requires courage.

But the biggest lesson is that leaders should not try to make everyone like the strategy. Instead, they should proactively build trust, which creates a foundation for people to accept and understand the strategic direction. Trust enables people to think, "I don't like it, but I'm willing to see how it goes."

The team's level of trust greases the wheels of strategic change. It does not eliminate the friction entirely but lets the machine move forward even when friction exists.

KEY TAKEAWAYS

1 Leaders should try to create authentic dialogue about the strategy. This means two-way communication and listening.
2 A goal of strategic planning is to build a shared vision by engaging internal stakeholders.
3 To enroll others and jump-start action, create a strategic principle and focusing question(s) that help others see their role in implementing the strategy.
4 Sustaining attention on the strategy often requires repeating oneself over and over. This takes discipline from leaders.
5 Engage directly beyond the top team since that gives you direct control over how the strategy is communicated.

WHAT'S NEXT

Many strategic planning processes stop at this point. Once leaders send an all-staff email about the plan, they high-five and return to their other work. But if you've made it this far into the book, you hopefully realize that a one-time communication is not enough.

Fortunately, the process outlined in this book is designed to bridge Strategic FUEL by creating a series of inclusive conversations in which people can wrestle with the strategy and figure out what it means for them. This decreases the likelihood that they resist the new strategy simply because it is forced upon them.

Because this communication happens throughout the process, you can continually test messages and frameworks that will make it into the final communications. By the end, you will know what will resonate because you will have already seen it work or not with various audiences.

Once you know those messages, you can use them to create a compelling strategic plan document, which is the topic of the next chapter.

Notes

1 Peter Senge, *The Fifth Discipline: The Art and Practice of the Learning Organization* (New York: Crown Business, 2006), 265, e-book.
2 Ibid, 276.
3 Sam Walton and John Huey, *Sam Walton: Made in America* (New York: Bantam Books, 1992), 315.
4 Orit Gadiesh and James Gilbert, "Transforming Corner-Office Strategy into Frontline Action." *Harvard Business Review*, May 2001. https://hbr.org/2001/05/transforming-corner-office-strategy-into-frontline-action.
5 Robert Debs Heinl, Jr. and Samuel Morison, *Dictionary of Military and Naval Quotations* (Annapolis, MD: Naval Institute Press, 2014), 20.
6 Carolyn Dewar, Scott Keller, and Vikram Malhotra, *CEO Excellence: The Six Mindsets That Distinguish the Best Leaders from the Rest* (New York: Scribner, 2022), 71, e-book.
7 Edgar H. Schein, *Organizational Culture and Leadership* (5th Ed.) (Hoboken, NJ: Wiley, 2016), 184, e-book.
8 Dewar, Keller, and Malhotra, 40.
9 Ibid, 81.
10 Ibid.
11 Adam Bryant, "Before Making a Big Splash, Learn to Swim," *The New York Times*, September 12, 2010. www.nytimes.com/2010/09/12/business/12corner.html.
12 Adam Bryant, "Leadership Without a Secret Code," *The New York Times*, November 1, 2009. www.nytimes.com/2009/11/01/business/01corner.html.
13 Dewar, Keller, and Malhotra, 123.
14 Ibid, 124.
15 Ibid, 125.
16 Harvard Business Review, *HBR's 10 Must Reads on Strategy 2-Volume Collection* (Boston, MA: Harvard Business Review Press, 2011), 34.

References

Adam Bryant, "Before Making a Big Splash, Learn to Swim," *The New York Times*, September 12, 2010. www.nytimes.com/2010/09/12/business/12corner.html.
Adam Bryant, "Leadership Without a Secret Code," *The New York Times*, November 1, 2009. www.nytimes.com/2009/11/01/business/01corner.html.
Robert Debs Heinl, Jr. and Samuel Morison, *Dictionary of Military and Naval Quotations* (Annapolis, MD: Naval Institute Press, 2014), 20.
Carolyn Dewar, Scott Keller, and Vikram Malhotra, *CEO Excellence: The Six Mindsets That Distinguish the Best Leaders from the Rest* (New York: Scribner, 2022), 71, e-book.

Orit Gadiesh and James Gilbert, "Transforming Corner-Office Strategy into Frontline Action." *Harvard Business Review*, May2001. https://hbr.org/2001/05/transform ing-corner-office-strategy-into-frontline-action.

Harvard Business Review, *HBR's 10 Must Reads on Strategy 2-Volume Collection* (Boston, MA: Harvard Business Review Press, 2011), 34.

Edgar H. Schein, *Organizational Culture and Leadership, 5th Edition* (Hoboken, NJ: Wiley, 2016), 184, e-book.

Peter Senge, *The Fifth Discipline: The Art and Practice of the Learning Organization* (New York: Crown Business, 2006), 265, e-book.

Sam Walton and John Huey, *Sam Walton: Made in America* (New York: Bantam Books, 1992), 315.

Chapter 8

A Strategic Plan Document That Communicates the Strategy Well

Don't be offended when no one reads your entire strategic plan. It's not personal.

Very few people will read the plan document from start to finish. Still, the plan document can be an important artifact of the planning process and, if crafted well, can be something your team comes back to regularly.

THE CONTENTS OF THE STRATEGIC PLAN

This section describes the typical contents of a strategic plan document. It is a useful framework for the information you need, but your plan may vary in form or emphasis based on the audience.

Message from the Board Chair and/or CEO

Where present, this section communicates critical context and broad themes for the strategic plan, which sets the stage for the content to follow. It should shape the narrative and how you would like people to interpret the strategic plan.

Mission, Vision, and Values

Most strategic plan documents include the organization's mission statement and vision to frame the strategy.

Some organizations also list their values in the plan document, though this is optional. It is most important to include the values if they have changed—e.g., to better support achieving the mission.

Description of Process or Findings

Some strategic plans also describe the process by which the organization developed the strategy. This may be important where the organization must signal rigor and inclusion—e.g., "We talked with the following organizations

DOI: 10.4324/9781003499619-12

and stakeholders, so we believe that we were inclusive in the process." But in general, few will care about the process itself.

Especially if the proposed strategy requires shifting stakeholders' perspectives about fundamental matters or envisions a new direction for the organization, it is worth spelling out the key parts of the logic.

For example, you might have content with titles like:

- "Research Findings: Challenges on the Horizon"
- "The Changing Picture of Hunger and Homelessness in Our City"
- "What's Holding Us Back from Doubling Our Impact"
- "Why Good Isn't Good Enough"

The task is to expose the underlying strategic logic to internal and external stakeholders.

Strategic Priorities and Initiatives

This content gets to the meat of what the organization will seek to accomplish.

The Strategic Goals or Strategic Priorities should answer the question: *What is most important to accomplish as an organization in the next 12–18 months to advance toward our vision?*

For clarity, the parts of that phrasing are worth examining:

- *What's most important…* : There should be a small number of priorities.
- *… to accomplish:* The priorities should be phrased as concrete outcomes. The vision may be lofty, but the most compelling priorities should be things where you can objectively assess whether or not you have accomplished them.
- *… as an organization:* Because of their importance, these goals are likely cross-functional and require everyone's buy-in and movement in the same direction.
- *… in the next 12–18 months:* However you describe the time frame, the goal should be time-bound and generate urgency. The deadline for achieving the goal requires shifting effort, attention, and activities. Without a deadline, there's no specific reason to take action today.
- *… to advance toward our vision?:* The priorities should move the organization in the right direction.

Typically, each strategic goal or priority will have the following information described underneath it:

A Why This is Important

Let's imagine a hypothetical strategic priority for a food pantry: "Increase Capacity to Serve."

The statement of importance might sound something like this: "Over the last few years, the number of people in our community experiencing hunger has increased by 50 percent, but our capacity to store and deliver food has been a limit to our ability to expand our service."

The reason to include such a statement is so the priority connects to the organization's larger mission and key opportunities and challenges. This is especially important when the priority requires organizational change. Without articulating the rationale for the priority, it may not be clear to people in the organization why it is worth the effort to do things differently.

B Intended Outcomes

State what observable, high-level outcomes you would expect to see if accomplishing this goal or priority. In the food pantry example, this might be: "We intend to increase capacity at existing facilities by 50 percent and build two new facilities within three years."

These outcomes may be related to quantitative or qualitative measures tracked during strategic routines. However, it is not always necessary to define the metrics specifically. It is more important that the broad magnitudes—e.g., "double the customer retention rate" or "raise an endowment of $10–15 million in the next three years"—signal the size of the task. You don't want people thinking of small tweaks when big changes are necessary.

The other reason to opt for broad magnitudes rather than specific metrics is that the former are typically more compelling. For example, "cut employee attrition by half" sounds like a big goal that everyone—including me—needs to focus on. In contrast, "reduce employee attrition by 3–5 percent" may be harder to understand or drive people to think about the numbers rather than the spirit of the work.

C Strategic Initiatives

These describe the activities required to achieve the intended outcomes. For the food pantry, we might imagine a set of initiatives (with the name of the person responsible) like:

- Secure initial support from at least three (ideally, all five) city councilmembers for expansion plans (M. Fields)
- Raise $1 million within 18 months (S. Smith)
- Hire a design firm to plan renovations/expansions of existing facilities by December 31 (A. Phillips)

The list of initiatives does not need to be exhaustive, especially at the start of implementation. The most important part of this section is to show readers of the plan that there are concrete steps toward the intended outcomes and who will be driving the work.

Financial Implications

Depending on the nature of the strategic change, this section may or may not be required. For example, if the implications of the new strategy are minor revisions to the focus and activities of existing staff or if the organization's economic model will not change, it is not necessary to spell out the complete finances in the strategic plan. (Hopefully, someone in Finance is doing the math to understand the budget implications.)

However, you should capture the *major* financial implications of the plan— e.g., the cost of hiring more staff, investments, and shifts in budget from activity X to activity Y—in the document. This is about ensuring that you understand the implications and a method of communicating the tradeoffs the organization will have to make going forward.

Enabling Mechanisms

This information may not be included in a public-facing document, but it's important for internal audiences. When the plan is created, there's often a question in employees' minds about how "real" it is. This is especially true when leaders (past or present) have communicated plans or change initiatives without following through.

Hence, it's essential to give the plan credibility by showing how things will be different. That might include things like:

- New organizational routines
- Investments that have been or will be made
- Activities that will start or stop

"Is there a specific format needed for the strategic plan?"

While most plans will include most of this information, there's no single best format for the plan document. It is best to structure the document to be relevant to your most important audiences, which will vary by organization.

For example, the organization may have an external-facing plan oriented toward donors. This might be heavy on stories of the people the organization serves, lofty language, great design, and engaging formats like a website or videos. At the same time, their internal-facing strategic plan might be a simple Word document that is more detail-oriented and focused on the *how*.

That's the difference between the plan as a reflection of the strategy and the plan as a communications tool. Both are relevant, but the use cases are different.

> "I thought I was brilliant, but [my boss] took me aside and upbraided me. It didn't matter how smart my plan was if the team couldn't execute it! It was a lesson that would serve me well."[1]
>
> — Captain L. David Marquet, ret., *Turn the Ship Around!*

MAKING THE PLAN DOCUMENT MORE COMPELLING

Tactic 1: Nail the Introduction and Headlines

When writing the plan, think about the various internal and external audiences for it. For some, the plan will be like a set of architectural plans for a house—they will look at the details to see how it all works technically. For others, it will be about the pretty picture of the house once it's built. Tactically, that may be having multiple versions of the plan.

Most importantly, **don't rely on people to read the entire document!**

Instead, use a meaty introduction and graphics upfront to capture the main parts of the narrative.

Then, focus on getting the headlines right. This is how many people will remember the plan. Ensure that these are clear and compelling.

The basic test: If you read the headline to someone unfamiliar with the organization, would they get the strategy?

Alternatively, think: *How would I describe it to an 8-year-old?* The language you would use is likely clearer and more compelling.

Tactic 2: Say Clearly What Is Different

For most nonprofits, strategic planning does not yield a strategy that is 180 degrees different from what they are already doing. Instead, the "new" strategy is more about points of emphasis. For this reason, it can be hard for people to understand what's most important or if anything is changing.

To drive greater clarity, consider having a section with a title like "What's Going to Be Different." It should include statements that sound like:

- Do more _____.
- Do less _____.
- Start the following activities and initiatives:
- Stop the following activities and initiatives:
- Hire [position] to accomplish _____.
- Eliminate [position].
- Shift budget from _____ to _____.

Not only will that help readers of the strategy get it, but it is also a good test of whether the strategy itself is clear.

Tactic 3: "Say It Like a Normal Person"

I once facilitated a strategy retreat for a business unit of a large financial services company. The unit had been recently formed to develop and launch a new lending product. Given that the team was rapidly marching toward their product launch date, the strategy retreat was critical for articulating what the product needed to win in the market and prioritizing everyone's work accordingly.

We designed several exercises to help them accomplish those goals. As we did the work, I repeatedly urged the team to "say it like a normal person." (That became a running joke, especially when, as the facilitator, I gave unclear instructions!)

I kept harping on that point, however, because of how important it is to enable a strategy that people can understand and evolve.

Because people interact most with others *inside* their organization, it's easy to have an internal orientation. Because of that, their language can start to reflect what the experts in the organization care about rather than what clients and external stakeholders care about.

The educators talk about the "scope and sequence" of the curriculum or the nuances of cohort-specific test scores. Parents, however, are more interested in whether their specific kid is safe and learning.

The housing nonprofit might talk about the need to implement a better regional housing affordability policy. Its donors and clients probably think in the language of "more people in homes" and "rent I can afford."

For that business team, the challenge was to shift from prioritizing product features based on the engineering required to prioritizing based on what their customers would value in the product.

When we write the strategic plan document using normal language, it is to ensure that it resonates with external stakeholders and that it reminds employees of what matters to those on the outside.

Building Strategic FUEL: Communicating to people about the strategy with accessible language—both in the written plan and in verbal form—makes it more likely that everyone in your organization can use it. And by making it accessible, you can include more people in the conversations you use to drive progress against the strategy.

Tactic 4: Create Compelling Visuals

Most people will consume the plan in short-hand form. By visualizing key elements of the strategy, you can support the process of stakeholders adopting the core ideas.

Make the Key Analyses into Compelling Visuals

When I led business teams, I often got on the analysts about the design of their PowerPoint charts.

Some of this was a personal thing. When I get bored and have a few hours to spare, I can easily get lost messing around with design software, usually thinking about exciting ways to visualize data. It also drives me nuts—"can't concentrate on the material" nuts—when there are too many fonts or colors, or objects are misaligned.

But, my focus on design was rooted in a simple fact: People respond more positively to attractive visuals.

Of course, anyone who's lived in society for more than five minutes knows how true that is. A Porsche wouldn't be a Porsche with a good engine alone. It's a *Porsche* because it just looks better than almost everything else.

In the book *Outside In*, Harley Manning and Kerry Bodine give a compelling example of how stunning visuals helped influence executives at the American Automobile Association (AAA) to think about their customer experience in new ways. They write:

"Dann [Allen, an executive in charge of customer experience] could have documented his findings about AAA's product renewal experience in a slide deck or spreadsheet. Instead, he pinned up each and every email, bill, reminder, outbound call script, and direct marketing piece that a high-value customer would receive come renewal time on a wall-sized timeline. Dann shared the visualization—which quickly became known as 'the wall of shame'—with employees from the company's call centers, branches, auto insurance, home insurance, IT, and marketing departments and asked them to verify the experience. 'People were flabbergasted. They asked, "This is *really* what we do to our members?"' says Dann. It was this wall-sized visualization that helped his colleagues to understand the customer experience as they hadn't been able to before."[2]

So, to facilitate people's ability to engage the strategic direction, you should consider creating compelling graphics. You can start by identifying the three to five most important strategic analyses. To pick the critical analyses, think about these questions:

- What was surprising to everyone?
- What convinced us the most to choose the path that we did?
- What facts might be helpful for people in the organization to have in their heads as they implement the strategy?

Once you have those critical analyses, find a designer to help you articulate them most compellingly. They shouldn't look like you copied and pasted them from a PowerPoint presentation!

Create Strategic Pictures

In the book *The 3HAG Way,* multiple-time CEO Shannon Byrne Susko recommends creating "strategic pictures" to drive forward the strategic execution. These "pictures" can vary, but they are visuals that contain the major elements of the strategy (e.g., the core customer, a market map, and key activities) and are easy to understand. The ease of understanding—which requires a diligent effort to synthesize the main ideas—enables the pictures to be helpful as a communication tool. Critically, the pictures can also become the foundation for the ongoing conversation about strategy.

Luckily, getting started with creating visuals is easy. Susko writes, "Some pictures are simple, some are more complicated, but most can be drawn using boxes, lines, circles, and sometimes sticky notes."[3] In some ways, it may even be better to have hand-drawn pictures because they signal that the strategy is open to editing.

Avoid a Meaningless Visual

Just because people often interact with visual information more efficiently does not mean you should create visuals in the strategic plan. If you do not have a graphic representation that compellingly captures the underlying strategy, avoid using *any* graphics. You don't want people trying to interpret the meaning of the graphic if it does not have one!

For example, if all you have is the three points of emphasis for the strategy, put them in three nondescript boxes to communicate them. If they do not have an order, do not imply that there *is* one. If they do not have a hierarchy, avoid anything that would signal such.

Instead, use your conversations with people in the organization to test different ways of communicating the core strategic ideas. And in those conversations, you can ask, "How would you state the strategy?" In that back and forth, you're more likely to land on a framework that's compelling enough to turn into a memorable visual representation.

Building Strategic FUEL: The visuals are not just for the strategic plan document—they're for what comes after. Compelling frameworks can help you keep people engaged in an ongoing conversation about the strategy.

KEY TAKEAWAYS

1   The best use of the strategic plan document is that it creates assets that *continue* to be used by people in the organization.

2   To make the document compelling, (1) nail the introduction and headlines; (2) say clearly what is different; (3) use normal language; and (4) create compelling visuals. Think about the kinds of things you might post on a wall in the office. That is where the focus should be.

3 To facilitate people's ability to engage the strategic direction, consider identifying the three to five most important strategic analyses and visualize them in an interesting way.

4 If you do not have a graphic representation that compellingly captures the underlying strategy, avoid using any graphics. You don't want people trying to interpret the meaning of the graphic if it does not have one.

WHAT'S NEXT

All of the work so far is designed to set your organization up to create a truly strategic culture that can implement the strategy and keep it relevant over time. The next section addresses how to build routines that embed strategy.

Notes

1 Louis David Marquet, *Turn the Ship Around!: A True Story of Turning Followers into Leaders* (New York: Portfolio/Penguin, 2012), 12, e-book.
2 Harley Manning and Kerry Bodine, *Outside In: The Power of Putting Customers at the Center of Your Business* (Las Vegas, NV: Amazon Publishing, 2012), 96.
3 Shannon Byrne Susko, *3HAG Way: The Strategic Execution System that Ensures Your Strategy is Not a Wild-Ass-Guess!* (Shannon Byrne Susko, 2018), 153, e-book.

References

Shannon Byrne Susko, *3HAG Way: The Strategic Execution System that Ensures Your Strategy is Not a Wild-Ass-Guess!* (Shannon Byrne Susko, 2018), 153, e-book.

Louis David Marquet. *Turn the Ship Around!: A True Story of Turning Followers into Leaders* (New York: Portfolio/Penguin, 2012), 12, e-book.

Harley Manning and Kerry Bodine, *Outside In: The Power of Putting Customers at the Center of Your Business* (Las Vegas, NV: Amazon Publishing, 2012), 96.

Embedded: How to Make Organizational Routines Strategic

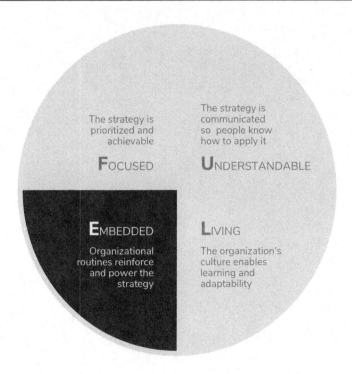

Get ready for the sexy part: organizational routines.

Strategy usually gets top billing in the planning effort because it's the forum for people to imagine the future and sounds smart with insights. But the real power of Strategic FUEL comes from the organizational routines that help you implement the strategy and keep it relevant. The next two chapters will help you build an effective and dynamic strategic management system that delivers on that promise.

Chapter 9

The Connection Between Effective Routines, Learning, and Strategy

How's your day?

Think about how you would answer that question. Now, consider your answer to this one:

How's your day relative to what you wanted it to be to achieve your goals?

The difference between your answers to the two questions is the same as the difference between those teams and organizations whose routines are strategic and those whose are less so.

Often, there's nothing wrong with the organization's strategy. However, because the organization's routines are not strategic, they cannot effectively achieve their strategic goals.

Let me provide some examples:

Financial Reviews: Have you ever read a financial statement and still had no clue what the organization does? For me, that is a telltale sign of a not-so-strategic financial report.

This typically happens when an organization uses generic revenue and expense categories rather than customizing them. The information is not designed to drive a conversation about what's working and what's not *for this organization.*

In contrast, in a strategic update, the data is granular enough to understand the underlying dynamics of the organization and is designed to provide intuitive hints about what to do next.

Most importantly, the conversations in these updates go beyond simply what the financial reports say. Of course, by definition, financial statements are the cumulative results of yesterday's decisions. The review is not strategic if the conversation does not naturally pivot to what the organization should do *tomorrow* to drive better finances.

Budgeting Conversations: One of the frequent laments in the strategy literature is how much time organizations spend creating annual budgets. First, the process is time-consuming, and no one enjoys it. But more importantly, creating a budget is often just an accounting or internal politics exercise that has no relationship to the overall strategy.

DOI: 10.4324/9781003499619-14

I experienced this firsthand when reviewing the budget of an education nonprofit on whose board I served. After reading the proposed budget, I asked, "What are we trying to achieve with this budget? What are the critical choices—what's in and what's out, and for what reasons?"

I asked those questions because, without identifying the strategy, there was no way to determine whether the budget was reasonable.

Operational Reporting and Project Update Meetings: The key difference between a strategic routine and a less strategic one isn't about the amount of detail provided. Instead, the strategic updates focus on what happened (i.e., the data) *and* what should have happened if we were successful.

The differences in those conversations are similar to the previous distinction between *How's your day?* and *How's your day, relative to what you wanted it to be to achieve your goals?*

Again, in the strategy literature and my experience with many companies and nonprofits, getting these conversations right is often the difference between effective and less-than-effective strategy execution.

This is why embedding strategy into routines is so important for driving progress.

EVERYDAY MEETINGS MATTER

> "You have the staff meeting. You do a check-in. Then everyone says, 'Okay, I've finished my coffee. I'm going to go back and actually do the work now.'"

That is what a leader who has been a nonprofit executive and a foundation program officer told me about some of the unproductive team meetings he's experienced. My guess is that you have experienced similarly useless meetings in your organization.

It is easy to excuse a single meeting that is inefficient, but when it occurs every week and takes up the time of all leaders (or the whole team!), it's a drag on the organization. More importantly, these inefficient meetings are missed opportunities to drive performance and strategic progress.

Even slight improvements would make these routines more valuable. As that nonprofit leader told me, "A staff meeting that solves a problem is a better staff meeting than one that reports out information."

But if you took it a step further and designed team routines to be strategic, you would have a system that fuels strategic progress.

Organizational routines are even more powerful when they embed learning. In the book *Learning in Action*, David Garvin writes, "A learning organization is an organization skilled at creating, acquiring, interpreting, transferring, and retaining knowledge, and at purposefully modifying its behavior to reflect new knowledge and insights."[1]

The most important part of that sentence is "purposefully modifying its behavior to reflect new knowledge and insights." That is how learning enables your organization's strategy to change continually and remain relevant.

"Achieving and maintaining strategic momentum is a challenge that confronts an organization and its leader every day of their entwined existence. It's not one choice a strategist must make, but multiple choices over time."[2]
— Cynthia Montgomery, *The Strategist*

WHAT HAPPENS WHEN YOU DON'T HAVE EMBEDDED STRATEGY

The easiest way to understand what you're trying to build with Strategic FUEL is to describe what you *don't* want.

As you read these less-than-optimal approaches organizations take to strategy and performance conversations, ask yourself: *Do any of these apply to my organization?*

Sporadic Strategy

Strategy is a sporadic event that happens only once per year (or, worse, every five years). Because of the long time between strategic reflections, the organization learns slowly.

Segregated Strategy

Strategy projects and initiatives are treated as separate from "normal" work. For example, the strategy does not come up in meetings where leaders discuss the organization's performance.

If strategic initiatives are treated as *entirely* separate from other work, it is more likely that:

1 Leaders will fail to give strategic initiatives the right level of attention or investment.
2 The organization will become overly focused on the present and lose track of the destination.
3 Leaders behave as if the strategy is someone else's job rather than constantly asking, "How is my team's work contributing to the strategy?"

Show-and-Tell Meetings

These meetings are reporting routines in which people describe what is happening in their part of the organization—while not doing the following:

• Focusing on what's most important

- Providing an assessment of what any of it *means* (e.g., saying how many clients were served in the last month without saying if that figure is high, low, on track, off track, within expectations, or outside of expectations)
- Identifying what they are going to do to address challenges and risks or to pursue opportunities

Hub-and-Spoke Meetings

The hub-and-spoke meeting often manifests in a dynamic of sequential sharing—one person talks to the team leader while everyone else is silent. Then, the next person speaks, and so on. It's a "team meeting," but it could just as well be office hours with the professor, with each student waiting their turn.

This dynamic works well *for the leader*, but if you ask others, they likely would not say it is a good use of their time. They probably also would not say the meetings help them learn about everyone else's work.

This dynamic can happen easily when there is not enough time allocated for a robust discussion or there is no clear expectation of collaborative problem-solving. It can also arise from a lack of psychological safety, which holds leaders back from raising challenges or saying, "I'm not completely sure about what to do; does anyone else have ideas?"

Fact-Free, Non-Directed Debates

This happens when teams and organizations do not have a concrete definition of success or their conversations do not include objective data relative to that definition. So the conversations become filled with conjecture, subjectivity, and ego (e.g., debating my idea versus your idea with no objective basis to decide which is most plausible).

This does not mean every conversation must have quantitative data. For example, the organization might aim to "have strong relationships with key stakeholders." It would be hard to assign a metric that fully measures relationships. However, if there is alignment about the definition of success, then there is a firm basis to say, "I think the relationship is strong because… " or "I'm worried about the relationship because… ."

"Too Many Meetings"

As former Intel CEO Andy Grove writes in *High Output Management*, "A manager … makes and helps to make decisions. Both kinds of basic managerial tasks can only occur during face-to-face encounters, and therefore only during meetings. Thus I will assert … that a meeting is nothing less than the *medium* through which managerial work is performed. That means we should not be fighting their very existence, but rather using the time spent in them as efficiently as possible."[3]

Despite the importance of meetings to leadership practice, people often complain that there are too many. But if you examine your team's meetings, it may be more likely that:

1 **Team meetings do not have a clear purpose.** The agendas are haphazard, and there is no way to judge whether or not the meeting was productive.

2 **There's no clear definition of what belongs in the team meeting and what should be handled elsewhere.** So, when people are saying, "There are too many meetings," they mean, "These meetings aren't a good use of my time."

3 **People do not adequately prepare their part of the discussion.** In this case, the meeting seems unproductive because participants do not know why the topic was nominated for the agenda, what parts warrant their attention, or how to respond productively.

4 **Some participants do not see themselves as a leader of the team.** And because of that, the team meeting feels like a disruption from their "real" jobs running their respective teams. Sometimes, a mindset shift in the participant is required.

Hence, it may be less important to solve for "fewer meetings" and more fruitful to focus on "more of the right meetings."

WHAT OPPORTUNITIES DOES YOUR ORGANIZATION HAVE TO IMPROVE ITS ROUTINES?

If you examine your organization's routines, there are likely many opportunities to make them more strategic. Here, you'll see some questions you should ask to identify those opportunities.

Results Management

These are the ongoing meetings to assess the organization's performance against important metrics and goals. They might happen daily, weekly, monthly, and quarterly, depending on the nature of the organization.

The relevant strategic questions:

- Do the routines (i.e., in these meetings) focus on the proper measures of success?
- In the meetings that make up these routines, do we identify the most important challenges and what we are doing to do about them?
- Do we have robust debates that help us arrive at the right decisions?

Information Sharing (and Channels)

These processes help people throughout the organization understand what's happening. This might include using one-to-many communications (e.g., town halls, emails), technology solutions for information sharing, and ensuring the work culture encourages sharing.

The relevant strategic questions:

- How do opportunities and challenges that do not neatly fit within one part of the organization surface to the relevant parties? Are those organically surfaced today?
- How can we reinforce the strategic themes and maintain organizational focus?

Financial Management

These are the processes to set and revise how the organization receives and spends money. For sure, this includes formal budgeting and accounting processes. But in the most effective organizations, these conversations happen continuously and are tied to the results management conversation.

The relevant strategic questions:

- How effectively does our budget and the conversations around it reflect what we identify in the strategy as most important to achieve?
- How effectively does our resource allocation change as we learn or confront unexpected challenges (e.g., mid-year budget updates)?

Employee Performance Management

Performance management processes are where individuals set goals; managers provide recognition, feedback, and coaching; and the organization assesses individuals on their performance. Obviously, organizations should have a performance management approach. However, for senior leaders, performance management rises to an organizational routine because of how tied their individual performance is to the overall result.

The relevant strategic questions:

- How effectively do our performance management routines—not just what's on paper, but how people experience it—help employees grow?
- How effectively do our performance management routines reflect the strategy (e.g., employees set goals based on their understanding of what's most valuable, and employees' goals change appropriately as the organization's goals change)?

- How effectively are we using recognition to support the behaviors and actions consistent with the strategy? (e.g., highlighting people who are making it easier to get work done or improving the employee experience)

Talent Management

These processes get the right people in the right roles. To use a sports analogy, performance management might ask, "How did Joe perform in his position?"

Talent management routines ask questions like, "What position *should* Joe play? Who is ready to step into his position if we lose Joe to an injury or to another team? What are we doing to prepare that person?"

Decision-Making

These are the beliefs and processes the organization uses to arrive at decisions. This often starts with outlining who has formal rights over what decisions. But beyond the formal processes, much of what makes decision-making challenging is when beliefs about how the processes should go (e.g., who should legitimately be included or consulted, who has the right to make the decision) do not match reality or what's required for the decision to be effective (e.g., timeliness, inclusion of the correct information).

The relevant strategic questions:

- What are the most important decisions for the organization to get right? (It's not worth taking on every process in the organization.)
- What decisions are most difficult in our organization?

Formal Strategy Routines

These annual (or less frequent) processes allow you to step back and assess where the organization should head. When an organization has a rigorous set of ongoing results and financial management processes, leaders are more likely to be aligned on the current state, the challenges the organization faces, and trends in the external environment. That enables the formal processes to be more effective and efficient.

The relevant strategic questions:

- How effectively do our strategy routines push us to think critically about the organization?
- How effectively do we implement the insights from that thinking?
- How effectively do we share strategic decisions and updates with the rest of the organization?

Learning Routines

These routines are the tactics the organization uses to surface learnings and new ideas and then disseminate and implement them throughout the organization. The relevant strategic questions:

- How effectively do we turn lessons into action?
- When there is an insight or lesson learned in one part of the organization, do people know how to share the lesson with others?

Team Building

These are processes through which teams learn to relate to and work with each other more effectively. Building an effective team dynamic supports all other routines. Still, organizations do not always have an intentional strategy to build the team dynamics they need (i.e., they take for granted that everyone will get along). The relevant strategic questions:

- Do our routines provide time and space for team members to build relationships and trust?

KEY TAKEAWAYS

1   When an organization's routines are not strategic, they usually cannot achieve their strategic goals. That's why it is important to start the process of developing robust routines from the beginning of strategic planning.
2   Inefficient meetings are a drag on the organization and are missed opportunities to drive performance and strategic progress.

WHAT'S NEXT

Here, we've just scratched the surface of why routines are vital to effective strategy implementation. The key thing to remember is that creating effective routines are about creating the right habits of mind and behavior—not just about the cadence and design of meetings. In the next chapter, you'll see how to design your organization's strategic system, but you should not lose sight of the leadership work of building the mindsets and behaviors to support it.

Notes

1   David Garvin, *Learning in Action: A Guide to Putting the Learning Organization to Work* (Boston, MA: Harvard Business Review Press, 2003), 10, e-book.
2   Cynthia Montgomery, *The Strategist: Be the Leader Your Business Needs* (New York: HarperCollins, 2012), 138, e-book.
3   Andrew Grove, *High Output Management*, (New York: Vintage, 1995), 71, e-book.

References

David Garvin, *Learning in Action: A Guide to Putting the Learning Organization to Work* (Boston, MA: Harvard Business Review Press, 2003), 10, e-book.

Andrew Grove, *High Output Management* (New York: Vintage, 1995), 71, e-book.

Cynthia Montgomery, *The Strategist: Be the Leader Your Business Needs* (New York: HarperCollins, 2012), 138, e-book.

Chapter 10

Designing Your Organization's Strategy System

How awesome would it be to shift the team from reactive to proactive?

How effective would the team be if, instead of being distracted by crises and squeaky wheels, it maintained focus on the strategic destination?

How much more impactful would the organization be if it softened the boundaries of silos and worked based on collective knowledge and collective action?

You can make these shifts when your team and organization implement a great strategy system.

The work to build that system, of course, is not easy. This chapter shows you how to approach that work.

THE ELEMENTS OF A MANAGEMENT SYSTEM WITH STRATEGIC FUEL

To nurture rich, adaptive conversations that lead to strategic progress, the system you build should do the following:

1 **Ask (and Answer) the Right Questions.** At the most basic level, this is about defining success and progress. Once a team has done that, it can adequately assess performance today and identify opportunities for the future. To have an excellent strategy conversation, teams should bring data—whether quantitative or qualitative, rigorous or anecdotal—to the conversation so there is a logical basis for making decisions. Critically, this is moving away from making decisions based on ego and power.

2 **Create a Set of Inclusive, Action-Oriented Conversations.** The power of a great strategic management system is that it can keep everyone focused on the overall strategy and keep the strategy fresh. But it can only do that if the strategic conversation is inclusive, generates learning, spreads insights across the organization, and then acts upon those insights.

DOI: 10.4324/9781003499619-15

The Process to Design Your System

I recommend a four-step process to design a strategy system that works for your organization. In the Appendix, you'll see a detailed description of each step. Those steps are:

1 **Identify the Right Questions to Ask.** These questions define performance and strategic success and, if asked and answered regularly, help the organization drive progress. Those questions might include things like: *How effectively are we achieving the most important outcomes for our mission?* Or, *How satisfied are the people we serve with what we offer?*

2 **Assess the Current State of the Conversations.** In this step, you'll identify if and when the questions are being asked today and how robust the conversations are. This will help you prioritize efforts to improve the strategy system.

3 **Identify Experiments to Address the Most Important Gaps.** This is the heart of the (re)design effort.

4 **Identify the Right Data.** For each strategy and performance question, you would answer, *What information would give us the best indicator of success or progress?* This step should come last because it is often the hardest, and you don't want to wait for the perfect data to improve the routines.

Mindsets and Behaviors to Make the System Work

It's not enough to set up a series of meetings or create a data dashboard. To get the full value from Strategic FUEL, you should be building toward the following mindsets and behaviors of leaders in the organization:

Coordinated Planning	Everyone knows and buys into the organization-wide plan. Rather than simply "adding" a series of department-specific plans together, the team seeks "multiplication" opportunities across organizational lines.
Transparency	We have an open, non-judgmental, data-rich conversation about where we are today. People do not seek to hide challenges—nor would it be easy to do so.
Commitment to Action	We take *personal* responsibility for improving results (not just explaining them).
Alignment with Reality	Strategic reviews and dashboards should match what leaders think about daily. If upward reporting seems cumbersome, or the data dashboard is used only in strategic reviews, it is a sign that we have not truly embedded strategy in the work.

TAKE ACTION! INSTEAD OF TAKING ON THE BIG PROJECT, GET STARTED WITH SMALL STEPS

There's a detailed process for designing new routines to make your strategic management system come alive—again, that's in the Appendix. But my experience with clients is that starting with that big project is overwhelming.

A better approach is to find small ways to start the process. Your work to nudge existing routines into more strategic conversations is the critical scaffolding for a more robust redesign later. These are the training wheels for what will eventually be your organization's winning system.

You can start with these actions.

1 "Top Five Projects"

The most robust management systems will have strong project management at all levels. But such a system also takes time to build. Instead of constructing it all at once, start small.

First, ask each team member to identify the five most important outcomes or projects they are leading. (This also allows the team leader to ensure alignment on what's most important.) Then, ask each team member to provide regular status updates on those outcomes and projects—ideally, in a public forum.

Eventually, you'll want to create a robust, strategic conversation about these items. But for starters, this will ensure a basic accountability for making progress on the most important efforts.

2 Start Meetings with a Reminder of the Strategy

It's not that every meeting should be a detailed strategy review, but every update should start with restating where you are trying to go.

That is as straightforward as starting with statements like:

- *We've historically paid attention to five measures of success, but this year's theme is Quality at Every Step, so we'll want to spend most of our time today on that.*
- *As a reminder, we're working toward being able to manufacture 100 widgets per month to support next year's expansion. Now let's talk about what's happened over the last month.*
- *As a reminder, our budget is only break-even this year, so we're focused on staying on plan in every category. Now, let's look at the quarterly financial report.*

If you start with strategy, the conversation is more likely to get to the heart of the matter.

(Re-)centering the strategy solves another problem: *not everyone knows the strategy!*

For example, new team members do not always know how things fit together. In nonprofits, board members engage only sporadically, so they might forget the strategy. And while senior leaders tend to engage in strategy discussions regularly, others may be caught up in the day-to-day operation of the business and need a nudge to get them thinking about the big picture.

3 Design for Discussion

The *least* strategic routines I've seen usually have a dynamic of presenting information to a senior leader, often with the implied assumption that the senior leader is either the judge of the work or the provider of solutions to problems. In contrast, the most strategic meetings tend to have a non-judgmental, problem-solving discussion that engages *all* participants.

In *Playing to Win*, A.G. Lafley and Roger Martin describe how they transformed the strategy meetings at Procter & Gamble along these lines:

> "*Slowly but surely, though, the review meeting became what we hoped it would be: an inquiry into the competitiveness, effectiveness, and robustness of a strategy. In due course, the presidents came to understand that they wouldn't be judged on whether they had every aspect of the strategy buttoned up but rather on whether they could engage in a productive conversation about the real strategic issues in their business.*"[1]

The other way this makes organizations more strategic is that it supports the development of junior leaders' strategic capabilities.

Lafley and Martin continue, "As a result, P&G leaders began to do more strategic thinking, to have more strategic conversations—not just at strategy reviews, but in the normal course of the business—and the quality of strategic discourse improved."[2]

I work with many nonprofits that struggle to build a bench of leaders ready to step into more senior roles. Often, the knock on junior leaders is that they are not strategic or do not see the big picture. Sometimes, these leaders do not know if they are ready for more senior roles because there are parts of the operation they do not understand.

Part of the solution to this challenge is creating organizational routines that are strategic and inclusive so that these leaders can build their skills.

4 Insist on Great Meeting Practices

Excellent meeting hygiene can significantly impact how effectively the team discusses the key strategy questions.

Consider these tactics to start:

1   Rename meetings so that the purpose is clear to everyone.

2   Ask about every topic, *What do we want to achieve? What does success look like?* Just asking those questions can be powerful in focusing the conversation.

3   List agenda topics as questions the team needs to answer. In *Harvard Business Review*, Roger Schwarz describes the problem and solution this way: "Most agenda topics are simply several words strung together to form a phrase, for example: 'office space reallocation.' This leaves meeting participants wondering, 'What about office space reallocation?' When you list a topic as a question (or questions) to be answered, it instead reads like this: 'Under what conditions, if any, should we reallocate office space?'"[3] When there's a clear question to answer, the benchmark preparation needed for an effective conversation is much more apparent.

4   Create language for shifting the conversation to a new forum. Having a forum for more extended discussion helps! You do not want it to become a way of saying, "We'll talk about that privately," or "We'll delay this conversation because it's controversial."

5 Make Your 1:1 Meetings Support the Strategy

Regular 1:1 meetings with your subordinates are critical opportunities to drive strategy. This happens when the manager clarifies context, reinforces strategic intent, helps remove impediments to progress, and supports the subordinate's development.

However, many leaders fail to make their intentions for these meetings explicit. They do not say, "Here's the conversation I want to have in our weekly meetings, and here's what I don't want." The first step in using these meetings to support the strategy is to clarify your intent. The good news is that you have almost complete control over these meetings, so you can design them however you want!

Unfortunately, time in the 1:1 often defaults to process updates rather than strategic discussions, problem-solving, and development that most leaders want (the subordinates, too!). So, as part of clarifying your intent, it is worth clarifying what information you would like sent ahead of the meeting to create space for a more robust conversation.

CASE STUDY: HOW ONE NONPROFIT TOOK PRACTICAL STEPS TO IMPROVE ITS STRATEGY ROUTINES

When a client of mine, a large public defender organization, started its strategic planning effort, the senior team reflected on the organization's progress against its last strategy, which was created seven years prior. The team quickly realized that they had not made much progress and that the challenges they faced seven years ago were the same ones they faced today. More importantly, they noted that the areas in which they made progress were those that had sustained senior leadership attention.

Because of those insights, they identified that improving their team routines to sustain focus on performance and strategy was at the heart of their new strategic plan.

The leadership team started by implementing several practical steps that leveraged what they already had in place.

1 Adding Progress Updates to the Weekly Leadership Team Meeting

For this nonprofit, adding weekly progress updates to their leadership meeting was an attempt to create a consistent conversation about impact and strategic progress. This was a shift away from using those meetings for the week's crisis—and with well over 1,000 employees and a social justice mission, there was always a crisis!

Critically, the update prompts were designed to:

- Create visibility on what work was in flight (e.g., "I didn't know you all were working on that as well.")
- Reveal opportunities for leaders to collaborate (e.g., "I need help with … ")
- Flag issues that needed focused problem-solving time

After those updates, the team would still discuss important issues, but the core performance and strategy were not lost.

2 Refocusing the Senior Team's Calendar Hold

The executive team members held ninety minutes on their calendars on Monday afternoons, which served as a placeholder for issues needing more time and discussion than the normal leadership team meeting. Proactively holding the time meant that the team did not have to scramble to find time for collaboration. Given the need to drive progress against this strategy, this time was repurposed for collaborative work on priority strategic initiatives.

3 Creating a Monthly Impact Review

During the nonprofit's strategic planning process, the leadership team held monthly all-day retreats to do the work. They converted this existing cadence into the Monthly Impact Review and Deep Dive, scheduling them throughout the following year.

The high-level agenda for these meetings:

- Review organizational performance and strategic progress (through KPIs updated in a dashboard)
- Department heads provide a detailed review of their strategies (e.g., Wins, Challenges, Risks, Opportunities)

- Deep Dives and Special Topics (e.g., problem-solving on important topics, tiger team presentations)

Tactically, the monthly impact review was also the milestone for updating the key performance indicators in the organization's new dashboard. It was also the target meeting for strategically important exercises like reviewing employee experience surveys and client feedback.

Starting Small Doesn't Mean It's Easy

This nonprofit started small with changes to how its senior team operated, but that did not mean the change was easy, or the impact came overnight.

For starters, the team did not have an existing goal-setting routine, so creating a robust conversation about performance and impact was challenging because those were not defined.

Relatedly, many executives were unaccustomed to sharing progress against their goals in a regular public forum, so they had to get used to the accountability that practice entails. For some of them, the hardest part was building the skill of delivering a meaningful update in less than ten minutes!

These more fundamental changes in the team interaction took time. During this process, the CEO constantly reminded the team that they were building new muscles and that she was building new leadership muscles herself.

The difficulty of making these team culture changes is precisely why you should start small and start early on building your team's strategic management routines. If you wait until you have designed the perfect system, you delay the team evolution and skill-building required to make the system work.

KEY TAKEAWAYS

1 Overhauling the organization's routines and creating a new strategic management system is a big task. Because part of the change requires many people to shift their behavior, consider starting small.
2 Starting early—really, as soon as you begin the planning process—gives the team a head start on strategic success.
3 The elements of an effective strategic management system are (a) asking and answering the right questions; and (b) creating inclusive, action-oriented conversations.

WHAT'S NEXT

In the next section, we'll discuss the final element of Strategic FUEL, creating a culture enabling the organization to learn and improve.

Notes

1 A.G. Lafley and Roger Martin, *Playing to Win: How Strategy Really Works* (Boston, MA: Harvard Business Review Press, 2013), 133.
2 Ibid.
3 Roger Schwarz, "How to Design an Agenda for an Effective Meeting," *Harvard Business Review*, March 2015, https://hbr.org/2015/03/how-to-design-an-agenda -for-an-effective-meeting.

References

A.G. Lafley and Roger Martin, *Playing to Win: How Strategy Really Works* (Boston, MA: Harvard Business Review Press, 2013), 133.
Roger Schwarz, "How to Design an Agenda for an Effective Meeting," *Harvard Business Review*, March2015, https://hbr.org/2015/03/how-to-design-an-agenda -for-an-effective-meeting.

Living: How to Build a Culture That Enables Strategic Learning and Adaptability

The strategy is prioritized and achievable

FOCUSED

The strategy is communicated so people know how to apply it

UNDERSTANDABLE

EMBEDDED

Organizational routines reinforce and power the strategy

LIVING

The organization's culture enables learning and adaptability

Chapter 11

What a Strategic Culture Looks Like

Let me tell you about one of the most strategic teams I've personally seen.

As part of a strategic planning exercise for a public charter school, I facilitated a conversation with the school's staff to understand their perspectives on the school's strategy.

Given what the organization does, staff members are much more likely to be deeply conversant in the language of teaching pedagogy, behavior interventions, and adolescent mental health than in the language of organizational strategy. Still, when prompted to think about the school's future, the team reasoned through the strategy as well as any team of MBAs.

One reason the staff could effectively engage in strategy was that they talk to the "customers"—students and parents—daily. Their understanding of what's working, what's not, and what else the customer needs is direct—not filtered, averaged, and sanitized in a report. Everyone knows it immediately when a kid has a traumatic event at home or a learning breakthrough.

So, when the group was asked to assess the fundamental drivers of results, everyone had a reasoned answer. And because they were constantly conversing, their answers about the strategy were aligned.

It was clear that the school's strategic culture was not an accident. It was built by their daily practices.

For example, the teaching staff meets at 7:30 a.m. to kick off each school day. In that meeting, they identify and discuss challenges they collectively face. But unlike teams in many organizations, these meetings aren't filled with pontification. Instead, the meetings are about crafting solutions the team can implement *that day!*

In strategy speak, this means they have an embedded cycle of test-and-learn. If the ideas work, they keep them going. If the ideas don't work, the following day provides another opportunity to get it right.

That meeting routine also gives the team lots of reps providing effective feedback to each other and highlighting issues without playing the blame game. The day I observed the morning meeting, the staff discussed a fight between two boys that occurred the previous day. The staff quickly deduced that the fight happened because a teacher—we'll call him Mr. Smith (not his real name)—briefly left his classroom unattended to help other students move to their next academic block.

DOI: 10.4324/9781003499619-17

What was terrific about the conversation was how the group moved beyond Mr. Smith's mistake. They spent more time discussing the broader structures that created a situation where Mr. Smith felt he had to leave the classroom. It became a conversation about *everyone's* responsibility to adhere to the school schedule to ensure the students were in the right place at the right time.

In other words, the school staff had a culture of psychological safety and learning that enabled them to grow from mistakes. Of course, it's not the easiest experience for a staff member to have his mistake dissected by colleagues, but it is made easier because it is part of a routine. It is just what the team does; they do it for everyone's mistakes.

Achieving that culture is facilitated by the fact that the morning meeting ends with reaffirming everyone's place on the team. They hold hands and confirm that everyone is valued and that they're on a joint mission. Because psychological safety is deeply rooted in our need to feel a part of the tribe, this is a powerful routine. They can have healthy debates because the debate will not result in anyone's excommunication from the group.

I left the meeting amazed.

After the session ended, I told the CEO, "This is exactly what every team needs to do if they want to be strategic."

This chapter is about how to create this kind of strategy culture in your organization.

THE ELEMENTS OF A STRATEGIC CULTURE

Let's first go back to what "strategic culture" means. It is undoubtedly **not** doing an extensive strategic planning process every six months. Instead, a strategic culture learns continually about what is working and what is not—and takes action on those insights.

However, that learning only happens when the organizational culture makes it comfortable for people to engage in the simple but difficult tasks of offering new ideas, admitting when something does not work or there has been a mistake, and entering into a healthy debate. Developing that culture requires leadership.

At the start of the book, I offered these prompts to help you get a sense of whether your organizational culture supports strategic evolution:

1   People feel comfortable sharing their challenges and performance shortfalls in public settings.
2   Leaders of departments proactively and openly end projects that are not working well or working as expected.
3   When there's an error or mistake, we study it openly without placing blame.
4   People regularly tell me, as a leader, bad news and ask for help *before* it becomes a severe problem.

Each of them is important, and here's why.

1 People feel comfortable sharing their challenges and performance shortfalls in public settings

This dimension of strategic culture is at the heart of performance. It's not enough for an organizational culture to *feel* good for people. For the culture to *be* good, it must achieve the organization's desired results.

Performance happens only when people feel comfortable openly talking about it. Imagine a business that spoke about everything *but* whether it was achieving results. That sounds like nonsense, but it happens.

In the book *American Icon*, Bryce Hoffman describes the state of Ford Motor Company's senior leadership meeting at the start of former CEO Alan Mulally's tenure this way:

> *"By the end of October, Mulally had finished explaining the [Business Plan Review] process and the meetings were going a lot more smoothly.... . But Mulally was frustrated. He had explained the BPR process and had explained the color codes. He had assured the team that this was a safe environment. Yet all the charts remained green. By October 26, Mulally had seen enough. He stopped the meeting halfway through. 'We're going to lose billions of dollars this year,' he said, eyeing each executive in turn. 'Is there anything that's not going well here?' Nobody answered."* [1]

The issue the team faced was that while there were plenty of challenges, the culture made executives hesitant to discuss them.

That's why everything on the status update chart was green. Their conversation only improved when Mark Fields, an executive who led the company's American business, took a risk and showed the status of a delayed product launch as red.

Only after seeing that Fields had not been punished for being honest did others start discussing performance in a forthright way. Hoffman writes, "A week later, everyone's slides were splattered with more red than a crime scene. There was plenty of yellow, too." [2]

This dynamic of avoiding honest performance can happen in any team. It is a problem, of course, because if the team cannot discuss openly what is working and what is not, there is no path toward improvement. This is even more important for senior teams because their challenges usually span organizational departments.

2 Leaders of departments proactively and openly end projects that are not working well or working as expected

This dimension of culture is the business end of maintaining a focused strategy. But why is focus so hard for organizations?

One reason is that adding "just one more" seems harmless. This is especially true if the "just one more" activity we're adding to our plates comes from a positive motivation, like *What else can we do for customers?*

Performance management systems sometimes provide incentives for leaders to add rather than subtract. After all, one gets promoted by looking like they're *doing more* than the next person, not by strategically *doing less*. What we miss, however, in that expansion of activity is that it comes with coordination costs that slow down existing activity. And if the "one more" uses up our collective slack, that can create other negative consequences.

In many organizational cultures, it looks "smart" to have a complicated plan. For example, in *The Knowing-Doing Gap*, professors Jeffrey Pfeffer and Robert Sutton write, "Appearing smart is mostly accomplished by sounding smart; being confident, articulate, eloquent, and filled with interesting information and ideas; and having a good vocabulary."[3] In that sense, having a simple, focused plan contradicts these incentives.

Maintaining a focused strategy is further complicated because choosing it means saying "no" to clients. Focus sometimes means telling some team members what they're working on isn't a priority. It's easier to let them continue that activity, regardless of the value. And focus may also mean saying "no" to powerful funders or board members.

There is no easy solution, but many systems that seek to create focus and an active culling of activity are based on building a common belief in the benefits of focus. Strategic leaders will always be fighting against the tendency to do more unless everyone authentically believes in the power of doing so.

Indeed, having routines that support focus is part of building that belief—i. e., it's just what we do here—but building the belief likely requires an ongoing campaign by leaders to win hearts and minds.

3 When there's an error or mistake, we study it openly without placing blame

This dimension of culture is about whether there is enough psychological safety to enable directed learning. This is important for mistakes—when there's a bad or unexpected outcome—and for innovation.

In her book *The Right Kind of Wrong*, Harvard professor Amy Edmondson defines "intelligent failures" as calibrated risks in new territory that help an organization learn. She writes, "Successful innovation is only possible as a result of insights from incremental losses along the way."[4] However, an organization that wants to continually try new ideas and strategies will be successful only if the culture identifies and celebrates the insights from these experiments rather than harps on the losses.

And when mistakes happen, the extent to which the organization will learn is controlled by how the culture treats it. Edmondson provides an example in the story of Julianne Morath, the COO of Children's Hospital and Clinics in

Minneapolis. When Morath implemented a new patient safety system, an important part of the program was to change the words people used to describe the actions that followed mistakes.

Edmondson writes, "Morath substituted neutral-sounding words such as *study* for the more threatening word *investigation*, which put people on the defensive."[5] That language change was one of several tactics to ensure that people could examine errors in the spirit of learning so that it could prevent them in the future.

> "Highly innovative organizations cannot stand still while remaining innovative.... Effective innovation management involves training people and designing teams to be willing and able to discard what they have become good at and become good at something else."[6]
>
> — Vaughan Tan, *The Uncertainty Mindset*

4 People regularly tell me, as a leader, bad news and ask for help before it becomes a severe problem

As a leader, you can preach about the importance of psychological safety all day, but you are in the worst position to judge whether or not the team feels safe. That is because the leader—the one in a position to assess everyone else—will naturally experience greater safety. The judge can say it is a safe environment in her courtroom, but the defendant surely feels differently.

Hence, to lead well, you need also to track the signals of psychological safety. Edmondson asks leaders, "What percent of what you hear in a given week is good news versus bad, progress versus problems, agreement versus dissent, 'All's well' or 'I need help'?"[7] When the news is weighted toward the positive, it may seem things are going well, but it could signal that people are not passing the bad news up. And that means the team is not able to learn and evolve.

STEPS YOU CAN TAKE TO START CREATING A STRATEGIC CULTURE

One mindset stands out as particularly important to being a strategic leader: Shifting from an approach of *I am responsible for the strategy* to *I am responsible for us having a strategy, and for everyone being jazzed about carrying it out.*

When I have coached leaders, the benefit of this mindset shift has come up regularly in discussions. The exchange usually starts with a leader's uncertainty about a decision. When I sense that the decision is weighing on their shoulders, I usually ask, *What would happen if you put the questions you're wrestling with to the team?*

My question is a test of whether those leaders are taking on 100 percent of the strategy burden, relying solely on their own ideas, or whether they are utilizing the talents and perspectives of those around them.

Sharing the questions you are wrestling with as a leader can also help because it forces you to confront the political and emotional aspects of getting a team to work in an aligned way more directly. In complex organizations, that is more often the barrier to strategic success than the existence of the "right" ideas.

Shifting to a mindset of *facilitating* the creation of strategy also has an emotional effect—removing the weight of the decision from the leader's shoulders. That is, it makes your job of leading easier!

The rest of this section explores the mindsets and behaviors needed to create a strategic culture.

1 Make Every Meeting a Strategy Meeting

I often talk with leaders who lament that their meetings distract from the "real" work. But from the standpoint of strategic leadership, all of these meetings *are* the work.

Every meeting is an opportunity to learn, especially when you ask, "How is the thing we're talking about here related to the big picture?"

Every meeting is an opportunity to reiterate and clarify the strategy for others.

And every meeting is an opportunity to "stitch together" the organization's efforts—e.g., to create connections across departments and resolve conflict between activities.

By treating every meeting as a strategy meeting—an investment in creating and maintaining alignment—one can create a team that operates more strategically.

2 Insist on Great Meeting Practices

I'm convinced that a non-trivial part of creating a strategic culture where speed, agility, and focus are prized comes down to something pretty boring: having excellent meeting practices.

Excellent meeting practices reflect a culture in which people are not just doing things to do them. Instead, people are operating with purpose.

When people pause at the start of a meeting to ask, *What are we here to accomplish?*, there's an implicit belief that some activities are a better use of time than others.

That's a strategic mindset.

It also sets up follow-up questions that are explicitly about the strategy. Questions like:

- *Why is this important?*
- *How does this fit?*
- *Is there a better way to achieve that goal?*

Similarly, when groups stop their meetings early to crystallize the next steps, they are actualizing a belief that real-life forward motion is the result that should come from meetings.

- *What have we learned?*
- *What decisions have we made?*
- *What are we going to do next?*

Of course, instituting great meeting practices will not instantly turn a culture into a strategic one, but they can make it painfully obvious where people go through the motions—i.e., meeting just to meet. And it can reveal where they are spending time counter to the strategy.

Our strategy calls for us to do X, Y, and Z, but I don't see these on the agenda. Can you help me understand the disconnect?

Interventions like those help strategic leaders create team cultures that are also strategic.

3 Keep Everyone Focused on the Outside

When talking to leaders, I sometimes glibly say, "If all you did was ask clients what they want and just simply did that for them, you would be 80 percent of the way to the right strategy." Of course, there's nuance—for example, "what they want" sometimes takes interpretation—but the literature suggests that is a good starting point.

The same point about asking clients what they want extends to employees and other stakeholders.

External perspectives are rarely urgent because most people outside of the building don't have our email addresses, access to our calendars, or the ability to walk past our desks. For almost everyone except the frontline team, most of the "urgent" items on our to-do lists come from *internal* stakeholders, creating a culture of internal focus.

This is the exact opposite of the culture required for strategic success, and the strategic leader will fight this tooth and nail.

The first way you can fight an overly internal focus is to have an always-on approach to external engagement and to insist that everyone in a position to influence strategy *directly* participate in that effort.

In addition to the information gathered, this direct engagement has another upside: it takes the ego out of debates. When you directly talk to clients, you don't have to rely on "your idea versus my idea." Instead, you can allow the needs of clients (and other stakeholders) to be the judge.

4 Increase Strategic Metabolism

Earlier, I used the analogy of metabolism—the process by which the body converts the fuel of food and drink into energy—for having effective organizational routines.

Because the high-quality fuel for strategy comes from consuming ideas and feedback from customers and external stakeholders, these efforts must be always-on. Jeremy Utley and Perry Klebahn's point from *Ideaflow* is relevant here: "You can't get ideas overnight. You need to keep them flowing in good times and bad. Ideas are solutions to future problems. They represent tomorrow's profits. No ideas, no tomorrow."[8]

The "efficient conversion" of strategy comes from all of the processes that help the organization turn those ideas and insights into action. For example:

- Creating individual and group time that enables strategic thinking
- Openly sharing emerging insights and questions you're wrestling with so that others can wrestle with them as well
- Building psychological safety so that people feel comfortable sharing ideas early and providing feedback to improve them
- Approaching every meeting as a strategy meeting to accelerate learning and keep everyone moving in the same direction
- Pushing down decision-making so that things don't get slowed down by hierarchical processes

The metabolism metaphor is helpful in that it reflects a *dynamic* system. Being strategic isn't just about having a good strategy at one point in time. Rather, it is about the ability to *evolve* that strategy as the organization learns and as external conditions change. The high-quality fuel of always-on external insights and efficient conversion into action enables that evolution.

5 Formalize Intelligent Risk Taking

Leaders can encourage the right behaviors through formal structures that give permission to be wrong. For example, a marketing leader mentioned to me that when he worked at Frito Lay, the idea was to use 70 percent of marketing spend on tried-and-true initiatives—those activities you know will work. But he was expected to put 20 percent of resources into initiatives that would push the envelope and 10 percent into true experimentation.

Similarly, in the Objectives and Key Results (OKRs) system invented by Intel's Andy Grove, the goal is to score 70 percent across your key results. The logic is that if people score higher than that consistently, they are not taking enough risk. In the book *Measure What Matters*, John Doerr, legendary venture capitalist and long-time board member of Google, writes, "Living in the 70 percent zone entails a liberal sprinkling of moonshots and a willingness to court failure."[9]

These types of structures add language that helps make experimentation and pushing forward the strategy the smart moves, which can lessen the sense of failure or inadequacy if an experiment "fails."

KEY TAKEAWAYS

1   "Strategic culture" does not mean doing an extensive strategic planning process every six months. Instead, a strategic culture learns continually about what is working and what is not—and takes action on those insights.
2   If the team cannot discuss what is working and what is not in an open way, there is no path toward improvement. This is even more important for senior teams because their challenges usually span organizational departments.
3   By treating every meeting as a strategy meeting—an investment in creating and maintaining alignment—one can create a team that operates more strategically.
4   A non-trivial part of creating a strategic culture where speed, agility, and focus are prized is having excellent meeting practices.
5   Leaders can encourage intelligent risk-taking through formal structures. These types of structures add language that helps make experimentation and pushing forward the strategy the smart moves, which can lessen the sense of failure or inadequacy if an experiment "fails."

The most important thing to remember about creating a genuinely strategic organization is that it takes time. As one example, John Doerr writes of Intel's experience implementing the OKRs goal-setting system: "An organization may need up to four or five quarterly cycles to fully embrace the system, and even more than that to build mature goal muscle."[10]

This is a primary reason this book advocates building a strategic culture parallel to strategic planning.

Notes

1   Bryce Hoffman, *American Icon: Alan Mulally and the Fight to Save Ford Motor Company* (New York: Crown Business, 2012), 121, e-book.
2   Ibid, 124.
3   Jeffrey Pfeffer and Robert Sutton, *The Knowing-Doing Gap: How Smart Companies Turn Knowledge into Action* (Boston, MA: Harvard Business School Press, 2000), 43, e-book.
4   Amy Edmondson, *The Right Kind of Wrong: The Science of Failing Well* (New York: Atria Books, 2023), 11, e-book.
5   Ibid, 256.
6   Vaughan Tan, *The Uncertainty Mindset: Innovation Insights from the Frontiers of Food* (New York: Columbia University Press, 2020), 227, e-book.
7   Edmondson, 291.
8   Jeremy Utley and Perry Klebahn, *Ideaflow: The Only Business Metric That Matters* (New York, Portfolio, 2022), 8.
9   John Doerr, *Measure What Matters: OKRs: The Simple Idea That Drives 10x Growth* (New York: Portfolio Penguin, 2022), 140.
10   Ibid, 34.

References

John Doerr, *Measure What Matters: OKRs: The Simple Idea That Drives 10x Growth* (New York: Portfolio Penguin, 2022), 140.

Amy Edmondson, *The Right Kind of Wrong: The Science of Failing Well* (New York: Atria Books, 2023), 11, e-book.

Bryce Hoffman, *American Icon: Alan Mulally and the Fight to Save Ford Motor Company* (New York: Crown Business, 2012), 121, e-book.

Jeffrey Pfeffer and Robert Sutton, *The Knowing-Doing Gap: How Smart Companies Turn Knowledge into Action* (Boston, MA: Harvard Business School Press, 2000), 43, e-book.

Vaughan Tan, *The Uncertainty Mindset: Innovation Insights from the Frontiers of Food* (New York: Columbia University Press, 2020), 227, e-book.

Jeremy Utley and Perry Klebahn, *Ideaflow: The Only Business Metric That Matters* (New York: Portfolio, 2022), 8.

Chapter 12

Seven Approaches to Driving Strategic Change

What might be the understatement of the century: Change is hard.

Leading organizational change is even harder.

Having a great strategy means little if you cannot get people in the organization to change their mindsets and actions to carry it out. This chapter provides seven critical approaches for leading in a way that enables strategic change, increasing the odds that you can deliver on your organization's aspirations.

1 RELEASE YOUR JUDGMENTS OF OTHERS

Less helpful approach: "Our people are getting in the way of change. They're so resistant."

More helpful approach: "I'm the one making others' lives more difficult by introducing this change. It's completely reasonable for them, as normal humans, to hesitate."

Leading change is a frequent topic I encounter when talking to leaders—both in my capacity as a strategy consultant and in my capacity as an executive coach. These conversations often have a judgmental tone. For example:

There aren't a lot of change agents on the team.

Most of the people in the organization are stuck in their ways.

I just need them to buy into my vision.

Or, put plainly, *Change would be easy if those bad people would change their ways and see the world exactly as I do.*

As you lead change, judgmental mindsets are not helpful because they do nothing to identify ways to overcome the challenges.

As David Pearl writes in *Story for Leaders*, it is worth remembering that change is your fault. "It's you that initiates routine-disturbing change. You are the one with the vision that requires them to stir themselves to action. You are the one wanting more for the team or business than it wants for itself. You are the one who has new ideas that upset their world ... ."[1]

DOI: 10.4324/9781003499619-18

Since *you* are the one rocking the boat, there's no use in complaining about everyone being nauseated.

Instead, it is more helpful to start with the assumption that everyone else is a reasonable person making logical decisions. That assumption creates the need to analyze *why* they are making decisions counter to the change you envision.

2 SHIFT YOUR OWN APPROACH TO CHANGE

Less helpful approach: "I need to be a good communicator and articulate why this change is good for the organization and its stakeholders."

More helpful approach: "I need to attend to the emotional needs of stakeholders and understand how their private interests are aligned or run counter to the change we need."

There are important differences between these two approaches. The former approach assumes there is a right answer that can be objectively argued. The latter assumes that "right" is subjective.

The former assumes that intellectual reasoning will get people to agree to a change. The latter acknowledges that humans have emotions that drive their decision-making.

The former approach assumes that the organization's interests are more important to people than their private interests. The latter approach does not.

My research and experience suggest the latter approach is more reasonable on all these accounts. The implication: If you want to lead change in an organization, you must think less like an academic and more like a pastor and a politician.

In other words, you must make the emotional needs and individual interests of the people in your organization central to your strategic analysis.

Of course, shifting your role does not mean abandoning "objective" strategic analysis. It also does not mean you can skip making a compelling, logical argument for the path you think is right.

However, shifting your role means you must acknowledge and accept that those tools will be insufficient to convince everyone you're right—especially those who stand to lose something in the proposed change.

That's life. And that's change leadership.

3 DON'T TRY TO CONVINCE PEOPLE OF A CHANGE. INSTEAD, ENABLE THEM TO CONVINCE THEMSELVES.

Less helpful approach: "When we announce the change, we'll provide its rationale."

More helpful approach: "I should share external context, performance data, and the strategic questions I'm mulling over with as many people as possible."

Often, leaders spend a lot of time crafting the perfect argument to convince their teams of the need to change. And based on how much leaders complain about the responses to their change proposals, they are not achieving their desired objectives.

Announcing change is like proposing marriage. If you're not 100 percent sure of the response before you start talking, you haven't done the work needed to be successful.

The problem is not with leaders' arguments. Instead, the issue is with their approach. It's hard for people to accept change and the hard work necessary to create change *unless they convince themselves* that change is needed.

Hence, your role as a strategic leader is not just making a convincing argument. It's giving people the information and time they need to convince themselves of the correct answer.

How can leaders enable others to convince themselves of change?

Avoid solo strategizing. Trying to come up with the strategy by yourself means you're not leveraging the insights of others. Importantly, it also means that when you come up with the "right answer," it will not be evident to others because they will not have had access to your thought process.

Always-on context sharing. When you learn something interesting from an important stakeholder, share it. When you observe a competitor making an interesting move, share it. When a critical deadline is missed because of a gap in how two teams are organized, flag it for those teams.

All of this context sharing closes the gap between what you know and what everyone else knows. And in that way, it closes the gap between what *you* think the strategy should be and what *they* think it should be.

Share the questions you're wrestling with. Many leaders believe they must come to their teams with the correct answers. However, there's value in suggesting the right questions and enabling others to think about them. Practically, sharing the questions means that when you announce a change, it will not be the first time people consider it.

More importantly, sharing questions empowers everyone on the team to contribute their ideas to the solution, which makes strategic change something *they* are driving rather than something being done *to* them.

Creating inclusive, strategy-rich organizational routines. The best place to drive this strategy work is within existing organizational routines—e.g., the weekly, monthly, and quarterly meetings you already have to discuss results and plan for the future. These forums are particularly fruitful for context sharing because they usually include several levels of the organization.

Designing these meetings to raise strategy questions creates opportunities for everyone to engage in setting the organization's direction.

4 DON'T ANNOUNCE A "CULTURE CHANGE" PROGRAM. INSTEAD, FOCUS ON THE DESIRED IMPACT.

Less helpful approach: "We're going to change everything you've come to know and love about working here!"
More helpful approach: "We're going to make an even greater impact on our mission—that's the North Star. It requires us to improve how we work together."

Because change is hard, a desirable outcome is required to help others buy into—and stick with—new behaviors. In the book *Organizational Culture and Leadership*, Schein writes, "[B]ehavior change leads to culture change only if the new behavior is perceived to make things better and therefore becomes internalized and stable."[2]

Another reason to focus on the desired impact: Your leaders are already busy. Amy Edmondson writes in her book *Teaming*, "Many change efforts fail because they focus on shifting the culture, and too often people at all levels—from senior management to the front lines of customer service—have a hard time making culture change a priority, compared to the piles of work they confront."[3]

Making the change real in people's minds is not just about making a great speech. In *The Fifth Discipline*, Peter Senge describes how change leaders he worked with came to believe grand speeches about change were a bad idea. He writes, "Gradually, they realized that it was like waving a large flag that said 'fad,' 'here we go again,' or, in the carefully chosen language of managers at … Harley-Davidson, 'AFP' (translated in polite company as 'another fine program')."[4]

Instead of making a grand speech, leaders should state the outcomes they are trying to achieve in clear mission terms. That helps make the change "real" in everyone's minds and on par with the mission-critical work they already have on their plates.

5 FOCUS ON SPECIFIC BEHAVIORS TO CHANGE.

Less helpful approach: "We need to change the culture."
More helpful approach: "If team members consistently displayed behaviors X, Y, and Z, we'd be more likely to succeed."

Culture is an accumulation of specific behaviors in an organization. Hence, the route to culture change is through behaviour change.

Edgar Schein recommends identifying specific behaviors to lead to your desired change. He writes, "If you want teamwork, what would team behavior look like and what kind of training and supporting structures would be needed to support such behavior? The more clearly the desired behavior is specified, the easier it becomes to identify the sources of learning anxiety and the kind of psychological safety that would have to be provided."[5]

In their book *Uncommon Service*, Frei and Morriss provide an example of how an effort to improve service turnaround at Ochsner Health System's Baton Rouge clinic centered on a simple behavior—saying hello.

They write: "When we asked Baton Rouge CEO Mitch Wasden what he thought the most important driver of significant cultural change has been, he pointed to the 5–10 rule. All employees are now asked to visually acknowledge anyone within ten feet of them and to verbally acknowledge anyone within five feet. This seemingly small change has made a remarkable difference in the urgent, time-sensitive clinic setting, where everyone has an important job to do quickly."[6]

Identifying the right behaviors to support your strategic change will come from questions like these:

- *What are the vital tasks or decisions we must get right (or improve)?*
- *What behaviors are required to do so?*
- *What current behaviors would we have to stop or alter? What assumptions or beliefs—explicit or unstated—are behind those behaviors? What are the likely reasons people would object to changing them?*

A Model for Behavior Change

Stanford professor BJ Fogg provides a useful model for analyzing the behaviors of individuals and creating potential changes to them. You can read about the model in more detail in the book *Tiny Habits.*[7]

The key equation to remember is: **B = MAP**

Behavior happens when Motivation and the Ability to take action are high enough when one receives a Prompt to take action.

Behavior

What is it—specifically—that I want people on the team to start doing? And what behaviors do I want them to stop?

When I ask leaders that question, the response is sometimes murky—e.g., "be more proactive," "innovate," or "be more efficient." Those framings are tough to get one's arms around.

If "proactive" is clarified to mean something like "they come to strategy discussions with ideas on how they plan to solve their challenges," it becomes a much easier outcome to design for.

Motivation

Assuming these are reasonable people, what positive and negative incentives exist in their context that make their current decisions logical?

For example, if the performance management system explicitly or implicitly tells people there's zero upside to doing something different from what's written in the operating manual, and there's only risk if you mess it up, then a team leader's encouragement to "be proactive" will not be impactful.

In a real-life example, I worked with one education nonprofit whose CEO wanted the director-level leaders in the organization to take a greater leadership role. However, the official "competency ladder" used to define expectations for each leader's performance mentioned nothing about contributing to the organizational strategy and impact. (It said only that they should "apply" the overall strategy to their work.) So, while the message from the CEO was for them to step up, the message of their performance evaluations was the opposite.

In these situations, leaders should think more about the following question: How might I change the broader context to make the behavior I want a *good* decision?

Ability

How easy is it for team members to practice the behavior that I want? How hard is it for them to practice the behavior I don't want?

When choosing between two behaviors, people will generally choose the easier one. So, as you think about leading behavior change, your goal is to make ideal behaviors easier and suboptimal behaviors harder.

Want staff to post-service reports into the system faster? Enable them to do so via a mobile app so they do not have to wait until the next time they are at their desks.

Want students to wear their school uniforms more consistently? Allow them to borrow items when they forget something at home.

Want everyone on the team to complete an important survey? Reduce the number of questions and ask them to complete the survey when everyone's already in a team meeting.

I have seen organizations use each of these strategies to drive important outcomes. In each instance, leaders could have badgered people about choosing the right behaviors to increase their motivation, but the most enduring solutions were simply to make the ideal choices easier to follow.

Fogg argues that changing ability has "the most power to stack the deck" in your effort to make new behaviors habitual because it does not rely on people's motivation, which goes up and down.[8]

Prompt

How and when will team members execute the behavior I want?

For example, a leader who wants more new ideas might start by ... asking for new ideas.

A leader who wants team members to solve their challenges proactively might add a box to the strategy discussion template for "How are you planning to solve the most important challenges?"

There are many other possibilities. I've highlighted these ideas because many of the solutions leaders develop to drive change have little to do with changing fundamental mindsets.

Instead, leaders can start by adding prompts like the one above and making subtle shifts in the team's processes and meetings to get work done. Often, it's not about getting people to *think* differently. They just need to *do* differently.

Mindset changes will come from behavior changes.

Before someone sees a change in real life, what evidence do they have that there's a better way than the way they've always done it?

Trying to change someone's mind through a meeting or discussion is like convincing your kid to like Brussels sprouts by *explaining* why eating them is good for you. It's never going to *sound* attractive to them.

The only way to encourage change is to have the kids try *just one bite* and let them discover that those tiny cabbages aren't so bad.

As people get used to new behaviors, they can change their mindsets. Edgar Schein calls this replacement of current beliefs with new beliefs "cognitive redefinition."[9] Once your employees can redefine their beliefs about the work and about their role in the work, it's easier to treat new approaches as "normal" rather than a deviation from how things should be.

6 REDUCE EMPLOYEES' ANXIETY ABOUT LEARNING NEW BEHAVIORS

Less helpful approach: "The change is obvious. Good employees should be able to do it."

> **More helpful approach:** "Learning new behaviors, and unlearning old ones, is a difficult and daunting process for anyone."

Most change efforts start with the basics—articulating a vision of the change, creating new policies, and training employees.

Those help build technical skills, but they may not address the fear that change triggers in many employees. Among those fears is that they may not be able to learn the new behaviors or will be judged negatively in the process of learning them. Schein suggests that overcoming this learning anxiety is about "increasing the learner's sense of psychological safety and reducing external barriers to change."[10] That means creating spaces where individuals and whole teams can practice, make mistakes without consequence, and get feedback as a critical part of enabling change.

An important part of making the change a positive experience is to signal that senior leaders are also working to make the change. When leaders share their own learning journeys and where they are struggling, it provides a model of success and creates space for others to take their own journey.

Leaders can also create space for learning by highlighting success stories from throughout the organization to show that change is possible and beneficial. According to Schein, what's critical is being "able to see the new behavior and attitudes in others with whom they can identify."[11]

7 TAKE A SCRAPPY APPROACH TO PROJECTS MEANT TO JUMPSTART STRATEGIC CHANGE

> **Less helpful approach:** "Where is the project plan to implement this initiative?"
> **More helpful approach:** "What's the easiest way to get this done and off our to-do list?"

I once worked with several consultants to support a quasi-governmental regulator with strategic planning. As the organization shifted from writing the plan to starting the work, we found ourselves repeating the words, "Be scrappy." The advice was to slim down each initiative and take an action-oriented approach toward it.

Scrappiness was needed to prevent every strategic initiative from turning into a *project*, since a *project* requires additional planning and implementation time. Because of their organization's purpose—releasing regulations after diligent study and inspecting companies to ensure compliance with those rules—creating carefully crafted projects was their instinct.

For example, conducting training was one of the emerging ideas for improving the quality of people leadership in the organization. That is undoubtedly a reasoned approach. I argued against that approach, however, because the actual work to create a training course can rapidly become the opposite of scrappiness. It often looks like this:

> *Identify the right person in HR who can design a course... .Well, it looks like everyone in HR already has a full plate, so let's hire a consultant... .Well, I guess we should spend a few weeks creating an RFP, and then interview people over the next couple of months to find the right provider.*

By the time the training starts, there's an excellent chance months have passed!

In contrast, the scrappy approach would be something like: "Let's just buy copies of *Radical Candor* or a great *Harvard Business Review* article for everyone and discuss what we want to implement as leaders."

That approach is less costly than training, and the first steps can be completed in a few hours.

Part of the issue is with how people approach the strategic planning process

Once a team or organization declares a formal planning process, it creates a framework of "There will be a time for thinking, and a later time for doing." And in that mode, the response to every challenge is to create a project to complete *once we finalize the strategic plan.*

The problem, of course, is that the end of the strategic planning process is often months away!

I advocate for reframing the *strategic planning* process as a *strategic action* process—that is, once the team is reasonably certain something is a top-three concern (i.e., there's 85 percent certainty it will be part of the final plan), the scrappy approach is to just start working on it.

At a minimum, this puts the team several months ahead when the final plan is complete. But it can also lead to more significant, faster impact by allowing people to "taste" and learn it before it becomes official.

Beyond planning, teams and organizations can also be scrappier as a cultural matter. Some ideas for how to go about it include:

Implement scrappier meeting processes

Ensuring every meeting has an objective and reframing "Discuss Topic X" meetings to "Make a Decision about Topic X" meetings would provide greater focus and increase the likelihood of action. The same goes for allocating time in meetings to identify agreements and next steps.

(These are also just "good meeting processes.")

By the way, the scrappy version of such an initiative isn't to roll out a big "meeting process program." Instead, it's for the leader to insist upon those practices in their own meetings—something they can start doing *today*—and let everyone else respond to that signal.

Identify and scrutinize delaying language

Organizations often have patterns of language that serve as delays to progress. They sometimes sound like:

> *Let's take that offline.*
> *Let's do some more research on it and come up with a plan.*
> *Let's run it by [the boss, the board, the committee] and see what they think.*

It's not that any of these are unreasonable steps—but they may be mechanisms for delaying action.

One path toward addressing these patterns is to identify the common statements that cause delays within your team and organization. The goal isn't to ban those phrases but to instead use their expression to scrutinize how scrappy the team is. That might sound like:

> *What's holding us back from deciding now?*
> *What exactly is the information we need to proceed?*
> *Are we checking with Susan because it's her decision, or is there another reason?*
> *Do we need to clarify the decision process in the future?*

Ask: How would we do this if we only had two hours and $0 to come up with an experiment?

Hint: Whatever the answer, try that first!

In some ways, this is a classic approach to agile design processes. It is an ethic focused on seeing if the duct-tape solution works before investing more time and resources into a more complex or lasting solution.

KEY TAKEAWAYS

1   If you want to drive change, it is more helpful to start with the assumption that everyone else is a reasonable person making logical decisions. That assumption creates the need to analyze *why* they are making decisions counter to the change you envision. You must think less like an academic and more like a pastor and a politician—i.e., make the emotional needs and individual interests of the people in your organization central to your analysis of what is needed for change.

2   Your role as a strategic leader is not just making a convincing argument. It's giving people the information and time they need to convince themselves of the correct answer.

3   Instead of making a grand speech, leaders should state the outcomes they are trying to achieve in clear mission terms. That helps make the change "real" in everyone's minds and on par with the mission-critical work they already have on their plates.

4   Most change efforts start with the basics—articulating a vision of the change, creating new policies, and training employees. Those help build technical skills, but they may not address the fear that change triggers in many employees. Leaders should attend to these dynamics in their change efforts.

Notes

1   David Pearl, Story for Leaders, (London: London Business Forum, 2016), 60, e-book.
2   Edgar H. Schein, *Organizational Culture and Leadership* (5th Ed.) (Hoboken, NJ: Wiley, 2016), 333, e-book.
3   Amy Edmondson, *Teaming: How Organizations Learn, Innovate, and Compete in the Knowledge Economy* (San Francisco, CA: Jossey-Bass, 2012), 345, e-book.
4   Peter Senge, *The Fifth Discipline: The Art and Practice of the Learning Organization* (New York: Crown Business, 2006), 385, e-book.
5   Schein, 332.
6   Frances Frei and Anne Morriss, *Uncommon Service: How to Win by Putting Customers at the Core of Your Business* (Boston, MA: Harvard Business Review Press, 2012), 163, e-book.
7   B.J. Fogg, *Tiny Habits: The Small Changes That Change Everything* (Boston, MA: First Mariner, 2020), e-book.
8   Ibid, 77.
9   Schein, 334.
10 Ibid, 328.
11 Ibid, 329.

References

Amy Edmondson, *Teaming: How Organizations Learn, Innovate, and Compete in the Knowledge Economy* (San Francisco, CA: Jossey-Bass, 2012), 345, e-book.

B.J. Fogg, *Tiny Habits: The Small Changes That Change Everything* (Boston, MA: First Mariner, 2020), e-book.

Frances Frei and Anne Morriss, *Uncommon Service: How to Win by Putting Customers at the Core of Your Business* (Boston, MA: Harvard Business Review Press, 2012), 163, e-book.

David Pearl, *Story for Leaders* (London: London Business Forum, 2016), 60, e-book.

Edgar H. Schein, *Organizational Culture and Leadership* (5th Ed.) (Hoboken, NJ: Wiley, 2016), 333, e-book.

Peter Senge, *The Fifth Discipline: The Art and Practice of the Learning Organization* (New York: Crown Business, 2006), 385, e-book.

Chapter 13

Your Role in Leading Strategy

The work to build a strategic organization will almost surely be wasted if those who lead it can't up their game to meet the challenge.

That's why this chapter focuses on *your* role in leading strategy.

HOW YOU CAN BECOME A GREAT STRATEGIC LEADER

First, a definition: by "strategic leadership," I mean the set of capabilities and behaviors that enables someone to lead a team or organization with a good strategy and the ability to evolve that strategy so that it remains relevant.

Being a great strategic leader is about two things:

- Creating a strategic culture throughout one's team and organization; and
- Building great individual strategic instincts.

If you do not do the former, there's a greater risk of leading the team into poor strategic decisions. And if you neglect the latter, it's much more likely that you will spend all of your time cajoling others to focus on the priorities while refereeing political disputes and resolving the conflicts that come from misalignment.

Here, you will find mindsets and approaches that will help you build your ability to lead strategy.

I BUILD YOUR STRATEGIC SENSES

Being a great strategic leader is difficult if you're not good at strategy.

It's not about being an individual savant. Instead, it's being able to say things to the team like, "We seem to be thinking most about [one part of the challenge], but we need to be thinking more about this other aspect." Or, "We should apply another lens to solve this problem."

Surely, reading books and research is part of building one's knowledge of strategy, but the learning process should not be a detached, ivory-tower exercise. Instead, you develop strategy skills by getting your hands dirty.

DOI: 10.4324/9781003499619-19

As business professor Henry Mintzberg writes in *The Rise and Fall of Strategic Planning*, "Effective strategists are not people who abstract themselves from the daily details but quite the opposite: they are the ones who immerse themselves in it, while being able to abstract the strategic messages from it. Perceiving the forest from the trees is not the right metaphor at all ... because opportunities tend to be hidden under the leaves."[1]

Practically, seeing the opportunities "under the leaves" means conversing directly with customers, external stakeholders, and team members up, down, and across the organization. It means purchasing competitors' products so that you can touch, feel, and experience how they work. It means having an always-on radar for ideas.

That is, directly engaging your senses so that you can notice the great strategic moves in real time.

Great strategic leaders don't wait for the neatly packaged, synthesized, and abstracted quarterly report for inspiration. Besides, a company memo is probably the *least* fruitful place to find a compelling idea!

2 CRAFT A STRATEGIC CALENDAR

Being a great strategic leader requires a strategic calendar. Unfortunately, our mindsets and environments often conspire to prevent a strategic calendar by providing a constant roar of meetings and to-dos that keeps us from regular, dedicated reflection time.

However, if you do not create the time and space to look up, out, and around the corner, there's little chance you'll have novel insights about where your team or organization needs to head. If you are always *doing something*, there's a greater risk that you are *accomplishing nothing*.

For some people, a good reflection routine might just be jotting down notes at the end of the day.

What did I learn that was important? What do I need to pay more attention to? What's lurking around the corner?

That kind of reflection needn't take more than a few minutes, but it can be a critical step back from the endless series of meetings—and the first step to synthesizing what it all means.

On the other hand, *doing something* with your reflections does take time. It's difficult to drop into creative, expansive thinking mode for an hour between a budget meeting and an operations meeting.

Hence, you should ensure that when you dedicate time for strategic thinking, it can be almost ridiculously long (e.g., at least half a day) and occur at a time when your mind is firing (e.g., not on Friday afternoons).

It may feel like a sacrifice to find time to reflect, but the investment can bring returns in the form of critical new ideas—ideas that are way more valuable than what usually comes out of the Tuesday morning budget meeting.

One of the markers of a strategic calendar is that it enables you to put disproportionate effort toward activities with the highest strategic impact.

When I think about the dozens of executives I have worked with as a coach and consultant, I would bet the number of leaders with a dozen 30-minute meetings on their calendars every single day dramatically exceeds those who have days that look more like three 120-minute meetings (even just 10 percent of the time).

The former is a juggler's calendar—designed around keeping all the balls in the air and whatever others put in our diaries.

The latter schedule—even if it occurs just a day a week—is designed to enable strategic progress by creating the ability to convene the right people to get meaningful work done.

When your team meets, do you have enough time to finish real work?

When I ask that question in coaching conversations, the answer is often *No*. Many teams' pattern is to schedule short meetings in which the assigned topic is only partly discussed—and they end meetings with a pledge to find more time for further discussion later.

Finding that time for more conversation becomes a scramble because the most senior leaders' calendars are already slammed. So, even if the topic requires just twenty more minutes to reach a conclusion, getting there might take days or weeks.

This slows down strategic progress!

In these cases, a better use of your time would be to schedule the meetings for *longer*—and get through the entire cycle of discussion and decision-making.

This is a mindset shift from "meetings" to "working sessions" and from "fit the topic into the time available" to "fit the time to what the strategic topic needs."

As the management scholar Peter Drucker wrote, an effective executive "knows that he has to consolidate his discretionary time. He knows that he needs large chunks of time and that small driblets are no time at all."[2]

3 HAVE CONVICTION, BUT HOLD IT LIGHTLY

Speaking on a podcast, Olympic and world champion track athlete Athing Mu described her race-day routine this way:

"I am the most easygoing. I am the most basic. I just want to make sure that I have my time periods lined up for when I'm eating, when I'm going to head to the track, when I'm going to warm up, when I need to be in the call room, when I need to be stretching... ."[3]

In other words, she plans to set herself up for success on race days. But Mu went on to describe how she holds that plan lightly.

She said, "You can't plan what's going to happen [on] the day of a big competition. I don't like to overthink anything. I just want to get there, be in the zone, be in the environment, take it all in, just kind of go for it."[4]

This is what great strategic leaders do—they prepare a plan for success and act aggressively on it while simultaneously listening to the environment and staying open to signals that they may be wrong and need to adjust. They have conviction about the strategy, but they hold the idea lightly.

So strategic leaders use words that leave room for maneuver. They are more likely to think in terms like *reasonable, plausible,* and *worth testing* rather than terms that imply certainty, like *right, perfect,* or *answer.*

They also communicate both the *why* and the *what* of the strategy so that, when conditions change, the need to shift is more apparent to everyone (i.e., it's not arbitrary or just the whim of the leader).

Indeed, most of the best management systems formalize this sense. Those systems are designed to clarify logic, align on the best ideas today, orient activity around those ideas, *and* set the process to evaluate and update that understanding.

That combination of communication and structure makes a group of people more strategic.

4 BE WILLING TO LEAD PERSONALLY

The most important aspect of these behaviors is that to be a great strategic leader, you have to *lead.*

The main reason why: Great strategy doesn't happen by magic.

Someone has to stitch together the disparate thoughts of the team into a coherent whole. A brainstorming session does not yield a cohesive set of ideas.

Someone has to put teeth behind notions like "focus" and "priorities." People don't voluntarily give up the projects that give them power, status, and potential promotions—their short-term interests—just because those activities fall outside of the enterprise's long-term interests.

And someone has to take responsibility for causing and cleaning up the complex political and emotional fallout from making those decisions.

Finally, someone has to take a leap of faith. Whatever analysis you do will *rarely* be good enough to describe how the future will unfold. At some point, someone has to take a point of view (even if lightly held).

Analysis is also never strong enough to say that sacrificing what's merely good to concentrate resources on the drivers of greatness—what Frances Frei and Anne Morriss call "dare-to-be-bad" decisions[5]—is a good idea.

In short, strategic leadership requires courage.

Using "someone" does not imply that strategy is a solo affair. It's mostly to recognize that strategy is hard because organizing human groups to achieve goals is hard.

Process does not solve the problem.

Committees surely do not solve it.

Legendary advertising executive David Ogilvy blamed committees for most of the advertising he saw that did not represent a coherent idea: "In my experience, committees can criticize, but they cannot create."[6] The same could be said for incoherent strategy.

The only solution is a leader who skillfully uses process and committees to get the group close enough to a decision, then carries the strategy baton across the finish line.

> "Effective executives know that they have ultimate responsibility, which can neither be shared nor delegated. But they have authority only because they have the trust of the organization."[7]
> — Peter Drucker, *The Effective Executive*

AN ALTERNATIVE APPROACH: BE A STEALTH STRATEGIST

It's a weird thing as a strategy consultant, but I spend a lot of time talking people out of strategic planning. The reason why: It is far better to be *doing* strategy than to be talking about strategy.

Usually, when leaders announce that they will have a strategy conversation, people start thinking and acting funny.

One of the first things that often happens is that people ask, "What is the definition of 'strategy'?" That is a reasonable question, but answering it is more likely to lead to a college-level semantics seminar rather than a helpful framing to develop a useful strategy.

"Strategy" gets people thinking of process—usually a process that lasts months and—painstakingly—involves everyone who might have a perspective.

Finally, using the word "strategy" usually raises the stakes—it sounds like something that will be chiseled on stone tablets and brought down from the mountain. Hence, people must fight over strategy, lest their department or pet project lose status or funding.

For all those reasons, it might be useful to think about another approach: stealth strategy, or doing strategy without telling people what you're up to.

It might be saying "Let's spend an hour logging and prioritizing ideas for *What's it going to take for us to be more successful going forward?* and *What's going to get in the way?*"

An hour-long conversation about those questions can often deliver 80 percent of the value of a "process" (not least because it takes time to design and schedule a process).

A stealth approach to strategy could also be integrating strategy questions into your 1:1 conversations. *I had an idea over the weekend about ways we might drive more impact. What do you think of that framework?*

After just a few of these meetings, there's likely to be a greater strategic understanding among the team. Whenever a strategy is declared, getting everyone on board with it will likely be easier.

The stealthy approach could just be bringing up the same topics in meeting after meeting. It's hard to ask the same question repeatedly without people orienting their work to provide a constructive answer!

KEY TAKEAWAYS

1 Being a great strategic leader is about two things: Creating a strategic culture throughout one's team and organization, and building great individual strategic instincts.

2 Surely, reading books and research is part of building one's knowledge of strategy, but the learning process should not be a detached, ivory-tower exercise. Instead, great strategic leaders develop their skills by getting their hands dirty.

3 Being a great strategic leader requires a strategic calendar. If you are always doing something, there's a greater risk that you are accomplishing nothing.

4 The most important aspect of these behaviors is that to be a great strategic leader, you have to *lead.*

5 When leaders announce that they will have a "strategy conversation," it raises the stakes, sometimes unhelpfully. Thus, it is sometimes useful to take a stealth approach to strategy—doing strategy without telling people what you're up to.

Notes

1 Henry Mintzberg, *The Rise and Fall of Strategic Planning* (New York: The Free Press, 1994), 256, e-book.
2 Peter Drucker, *The Effective Executive: The Definitive Guide to Getting the Right Things Done* (New York: HarperCollins, 1967), 49.
3 Ryan Clark, Fred Taylor and Channing Crowder, "The Pivot: Athing Mu World's Fastest Young Female in Track & Field History, 2x Gold Medalist at 20." *The Pivot,* August 15, 2022, https://youtu.be/UF1fzEikcdQ.
4 Ibid.
5 Frances Frei and Anne Morriss, *Unleashed: The Unapologetic Leader's Guide to Empowering Everyone Around You* (Boston, MA: Harvard Business Review Press, 2020), 127, e-book.
6 David Ogilvy, *Ogilvy on Advertising* (New York: Vintage Books, 1985), 32.
7 Peter Drucker, *The Effective Executive: The Definitive Guide to Getting the Right Things Done* (New York: HarperCollins, 1967), xxii.

References

Ryan Clark, Fred Taylor, and Channing Crowder, "The Pivot: Athing Mu World's Fastest Young Female in Track & Field History, 2x Gold Medalist at 20." *The Pivot*, August 15, 2022, https://youtu.be/UF1fzEikcdQ.

Peter Drucker, *The Effective Executive: The Definitive Guide to Getting the Right Things Done* (New York: HarperCollins, 1967), xxii.

Peter Drucker, *The Effective Executive: The Definitive Guide to Getting the Right Things Done* (New York: HarperCollins, 1967), 49.

Frances Frei and Anne Morriss, *Unleashed: The Unapologetic Leader's Guide to Empowering Everyone Around You* (Boston, MA: Harvard Business Review Press, 2020), 127, e-book.

Henry Mintzberg, *The Rise and Fall of Strategic Planning* (New York: The Free Press, 1994), 256, e-book.

David Ogilvy, *Ogilvy on Advertising* (New York: Vintage Books, 1985), 32.

Chapter 14

Final Thoughts

BACK TO THE CORE ARGUMENTS

At the start of the book, I made several arguments. I bring them back here to synthesize the main takeaways.

Argument 1

Most nonprofits approach strategic planning in ways that take too much time and effort, with uncertain impact.

The most important thing you can do to make strategic planning effective is to ask *Why are we doing this?* Answering that question and generating alignment among the senior team will help you design the planning process to address the most critical opportunities and challenges. It also will enable you to avoid wasting time on those activities that will not provide strategic clarity.

Argument 2

The BIG PROCESS approach to strategic planning is a good way to manage the politics of setting strategy. It will help you find an acceptable answer, but it does not always help you find the right strategic answer.

When the strategy calls for deep research or solving a technical challenge, consider using tiger teams of experts. They can move much faster than a larger group without expertise.

But if the strategy process is likely to suggest significant changes, you should treat the entire process as one of politics and creating alignment. At every step, including people in the thought process can pave the road to change. Tactically, that means you should treat the strategic analysis effort as a mechanism to help people shift their perspective, and you should communicate the emerging strategic logic widely.

This work provides the tools for people to convince themselves of the change rather than trying to convince them.

DOI: 10.4324/9781003499619-20

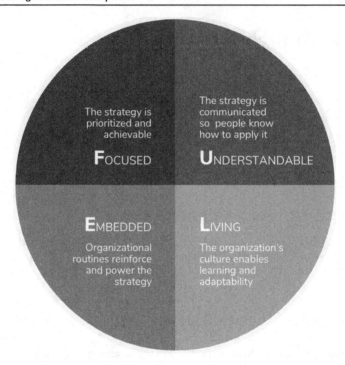

Figure 14.1 The Elements of Strategic FUEL

Argument 3

Needing to conduct a formal strategic planning process is a signal that your organization may not be strategic enough on a day-to-day basis.

You don't want to wake up three years from now and realize that the strategy you created is not working, so building Strategic FUEL should be the fundamental goal of strategic planning. It is more impactful to be learning and improving *continuously* because that keeps the strategy relevant.

However, building a strategic culture takes time. That is why you should start building strategic routines parallel to crafting the strategy. That gives you more practice and can accelerate progress once the strategy is set.

Argument 4

If your planning process is "develop strategy, then create an implementation plan," you're wasting valuable time when you could be having an impact.

Don't wait until the end of the planning process to take action. As you identify no-regrets moves, get them moving. This brings forward impact and provides an opportunity to practice the strategy routines and confront the realities of implementation.

You can also confront the realities of implementation by allowing the doers to shape the strategy. Their ability to identify potential hurdles and the trade-offs necessary for effective implementation sets the strategy up for success.

Argument 5

The best strategies have a "best by" date.

Setting a strategy is not the end of the process! Clarifying that strategy is built on assumptions can set the stage for directed learning to update those assumptions. And the robust, strategic routines that you create can drive this learning.

STRATEGIC MESSINESS

This book presents a clear view of success in strategic planning and action. But despite the book's logical, step-by-step order, strategy is always messy and complicated in reality.

My research and consulting experience on strategy and strategy processes leaves me with two main thoughts:

1 Strategy is easy. It's people that are hard. Unfortunately, most of strategy is people

When my son was younger, I would tell him constantly how awesome it would be for our household if he learned how to use the potty—time savings, cost savings, and significantly greater team morale. But despite my airtight case, if he was not enthused to carry out the strategy, it did not matter how well-crafted my argument was.

It's the same in organizations.

Getting the strategic process right is about building shared understanding, motivating, and then ensuring alignment between the human beings of the organization—in other words, it's all leadership.

Put another way, strategy is hard because leadership is hard.

2 There's probably not a "best practice." Or if there is, no one knows what it is

Organizations operate in vastly different contexts, so what's considered a "good" strategy varies. And even in the same context, as A.G. Lafley and Roger Martin point out in *Playing to Win*, "There are multiple ways to win in almost any industry."[1]

In the book *Hard Facts, Dangerous Half-Truths, & Total Nonsense*, Stanford professors Jeffrey Pfeffer and Robert Sutton write, "Those of us who hawk business knowledge need to come clean. We need to deny that we have magic answers."[2]

Let's consider an example. *In Search of Excellence* is one of the best-selling business books ever. Yet, when academics Michael Hitt and Duane Ireland compared the "best-run" companies to a sample of Fortune 1000 companies, they found few differences in characteristics or performance between the two groups. They write, "The research presented herein casts doubt as to whether the firms used as the basis for the Peters and Waterman book and for sequels it has spawned are actually 'excellent.'"[3]

Moreover, it does not take long to find literature—even from leading scholars—that recommends supposedly enduring lessons from companies that have since failed. Even the book *Hard Facts* contains one of these. The authors write:

> *"Kodak and Polaroid are perfect examples. Both had impressive R&D efforts and people who were deeply knowledgeable about digital photography, but Kodak's slowness to act on that knowledge has deeply wounded the company, and Polaroid's more pronounced inability to capitalize on its deep knowledge of digital photography ultimately led to its demise."[4]*

That story is meant to be a cautionary tale of being bound by existing customers and processes and failing to innovate. Of course, the book was published in 2006, a mere year before the iPhone made digital photography obsolete, so those companies were probably wise not to attempt the arduous task of building a whole new capability.

It's not that the popular strategy recommendations you've heard are necessarily *wrong*. It's more that strategy is so complex that there's no formula for success.

Does that cool idea you read about in *Harvard Business Review* work? Sometimes. Will it work for your team or organization? Maybe.

Or, as Pfeffer and Sutton put it, "We need to confess that we are just suggesting ideas that might make managers' hard jobs a bit easier."[5]

This book aimed to do that for you—make your job as a strategic leader easier. I hope it's done that!

JUST GET STARTED!

Setting strategy is the easy part. *Doing something* about it is immensely more difficult. I applaud you for even going down this path.

Now, let me undermine everything you've read so far. It's not having good ideas about what to do that matters. It's taking action on what you know. So, reading this book is a start, but the work continues from here.

Unfortunately, it's also non-stop work. One of my favorite statements on strategy comes from Sam Walton, the founder of Walmart. In his memoir, *Sam Walton: Made in America*, he writes, "When folks have asked me, 'How did Wal-Mart do it?' I've usually been flip about answering them. 'Friend, we just got after it and stayed after it,' I'd say."[6]

That is what the effort to build Strategic FUEL is about—the hard work, day-to-day, meeting-by-meeting, to push the organization in the right direction. There is no way around this work, but the reward on the other side is worth it.

Notes

1 A.G. Lafley and Roger Martin, *Playing to Win: How Strategy Really Works* (Boston, MA: Harvard Business Review Press, 2013), 88.
2 Jeffrey Pfeffer and Robert Sutton, *Hard Facts, Dangerous Half-Truths And Total Nonsense: Profiting From Evidence-Based Management* (Boston, MA: Harvard Business Review Press, 2006), 46, e-book.
3 Michael A. Hitt and R. Duane Ireland, "Peters and Waterman Revisited: The Unended Quest for Excellence." *The Academy of Management Executive (1987–1989)*, May, 1987, Vol. 1, No. 2 (May, 1987), 91–98.
4 Pfeffer and Sutton, 149.
5 Ibid, 46.
6 Sam Walton and John Huey, *Sam Walton: Made in America* (New York: Bantam Books, 1992), xi–xii.

References

Michael A. Hitt and R. Duane Ireland, "Peters and Waterman Revisited: The Unended Quest for Excellence." *The Academy of Management Executive*(1987–1989), Vol. 1, No. 2 (May1987), 91–98.
A.G. Lafley and Roger Martin, *Playing to Win: How Strategy Really Works* (Boston, MA: Harvard Business Review Press, 2013), 88.
Jeffrey Pfeffer and Robert Sutton, *Hard Facts, Dangerous Half-Truths And Total Nonsense: Profiting From Evidence-Based Management* (Boston, MA: Harvard Business Review Press, 2006), 46, e-book.
Sam Walton and John Huey, *Sam Walton: Made in America* (New York: Bantam Books, 1992), xi–xii.

Strategic Analysis Ideas

In the main part of the book, I described several areas of strategic analysis. Here, you'll see ideas for specific analyses that, in my experience, deliver the greatest strategic insight.

ANALYSES OF YOUR SERVICE OR PRODUCT

Net Promoter Score (NPS)

Measuring NPS starts with asking your clients or customers the following questions:

1   How likely are you to recommend our service [or product] to a friend or family member? [0–10 scale]
2   What's the reason for your score? [open-text response]
3   Is there anything we could have done to make your experience more exceptional? [open-text response]

The answer to the NPS question reflects the strength of their feelings toward the organization. The open-text questions provide information to help you improve.

Fred Reichheld, the former Bain & Company partner and creator of NPS, described why a recommendation is so personal and, thus, a powerful way of thinking about customer satisfaction. He writes, "When people recommend a product or service, they are effectively cobranding their own reputation with the recommended company. If a friend acts on their recommendation and ends up being unhappy, this reflects badly on the recommender's judgment and trustworthiness."[1]

While NPS may be an interesting data point to *start* measuring during strategy processes, it's best used as part of a system and organizational focus on delighting stakeholders. When you regularly measure net promoter scores and ask your stakeholders what the organization could have done to make their experience better, it gives you the chance to continually improve.

Other Insightful Analyses

- **Attribute Analysis: What Do Clients Value?** This analysis is about grounding the organization in what clients and donors want from the organization. If an organization is not constantly asking what these stakeholders value, there can be a gap between what they want and what the organization delivers. And that mismatch can cause a misallocation of time and effort. You can identify the specific services and attributes of each service that matter most via surveys, empathy interviews, focus groups, and studying your organization's data.

- **Journey Map.** A journey map tracks how clients, recipients, customers, or donors interact with your organization. It can be insightful because it requires seeing those interactions from *their* perspectives and understanding what they want at each step. When done well, this analysis can help identify critical gaps and opportunities to improve experiences—many of which may otherwise go unnoticed by people inside the organization.

ANALYSES OF EMPLOYEES AND THEIR EXPERIENCES

Employee Net Promoter Score (eNPS)

Employee Net Promoter Score is based on employees' responses to, "How likely are you to recommend the organization as a place to work to a friend or family member?" Their answers reflect the strength of their attachment to the organization.

The section contains visuals of analyses I've done for organizations previously.

Psychological Safety

Amy Edmondson states, "Psychological safety is broadly defined as a climate in which people are comfortable expressing and being themselves. More specifically, when people have psychological safety at work, they feel comfortable sharing concerns and mistakes without fear of embarrassment or retribution." [2]

High safety is essential for organizational learning. For this reason, it is critical for effective ongoing strategy routines.

Measuring psychological safety in the organization entails asking people how much they would agree with these seven prompts from Edmondson[3]:

1 If you make a mistake on this team, it is often held against you.
2 Members of this team are able to bring up problems and tough issues.
3 People on this team sometimes reject others for being different.
4 It is safe to take a risk on this team.
5 It is difficult to ask other members of this team for help.
6 No one on this team would deliberately act in a way that undermines my efforts.
7 Working with members of this team, my unique skills and talents are valued and utilized.

(Note: Items 1, 3, and 5 are stated negatively, so they would be scored on a reverse scale.)

Share of employees indicating each category

(Responses on a 0-10 scale. Promoters: those answering 9-10. Passives: those answering 7-8.
Detractors: those responding 0-6)

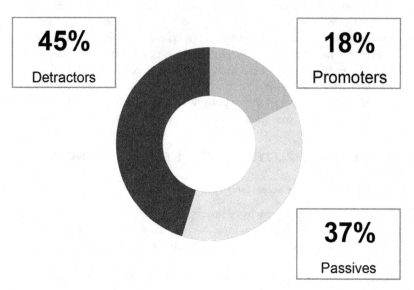

| 45%
Detractors | | 18%
Promoters |

37%
Passives

Figure A1 Net Promoter Score Responses

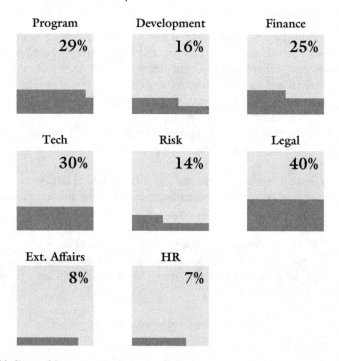

Figure A2 Share of Promoters by Department

Employee Engagement and Intent to Stay

Gallup has developed twelve questions to measure employee engagement.[4] This framework is helpful because it's grounded in research, and research shows higher engagement to be associated with lower absenteeism, lower turnover, lower incidence of safety incidents, higher productivity, and higher customer metrics and sales.[5]

Figure A4 shows how this data looked for one nonprofit organization. It used their answers to the engagement questions and a question about whether employees saw themselves working at the organization in three years to shed light on the organization's attrition challenge.

Attribute Map: What Do Employees Value?

Identifying what employees most want from their experience in the organization can be important to increasing satisfaction and retention. In many organizations, there's an unstated belief about what employees value, but there is no ongoing measurement. This analysis aims to bring clarity to this question and identify those dimensions in which improvement would be most valuable.

Other Insightful Analyses

- **HR Data Deep Dive.** Organizations can mine existing HR data for evidence of employee experience successes or challenges—e.g., attrition, performance ratings, promotion rates.
- **Job Design & Complexity.** In *Uncommon Service*, Frances Frei and Anne Morriss describe how some effectiveness challenges come from employees' jobs becoming more complex over time. They write, "[T]he average employee is drowning in complexity. And the outstanding employee, the one who has a chance of keeping up, is a much scarcer resource than many managers are willing to acknowledge. We're designing jobs for superhumans, and it turns out our people are flesh

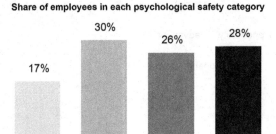

Share of employees in each psychological safety category

Low 7-20	Moderate 21-27	High 28-31	Very High 32-35
17%	30%	26%	28%

Figure A3 Employee Reports of Psychological Safety

	Committed Completely or somewhat anticipate staying here	**Uncommitted** Neutral or do not anticipate staying here
Engaged 4+ engagement score	36%	18%
Somewhat Engaged 3-4 engagement score	11%	22%
Disengaged <3 engagement score	2%	11%

Figure A4 Employee Engagement and Intention to Stay at the Organization

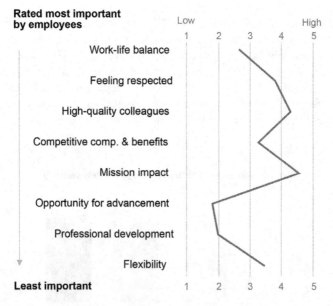

Average employee ratings on each attribute of employment

Figure A5 Employee Value Proposition Attribute Map

and blood."[6] The solution is to analyze whether roles are appropriately designed for employees to be successful.

WATCH OUT: ASKING "STRATEGY" QUESTIONS IN EMPLOYEE SURVEYS

Outside of questions directed at employees' experiences, organizations doing surveys in the context of their strategic planning often want to ask about, well, strategy. This also sometimes sounds like, "If we don't ask for their views on strategy, people won't believe their voices are heard."

There are two problems with this approach.

First, if you do not have a truly inclusive way of working, asking people what they think and returning to your typical non-inclusive approach will not make them feel better about the strategy. The survey will not make them magically believe their voices are heard if nothing changes.

Second—*I almost want to whisper this*—employees' answers to strategy questions usually are not that insightful. I once conducted an all-staff survey of a nonprofit that served as a quasi-governmental regulator. The organization's leaders insisted on including open-ended questions for staff about the strategy, like *From a strategy perspective, what are the one to three most important opportunities for the organization right now?*

When analyzing the responses, at least 75 percent of the suggestions were not about strategy. Instead, they were suggestions on how to make employees' lives better!

(Of course, employees' perspectives about improving their experience are important. But these perspectives should be collected continuously, separate from strategy processes.)

If the organization is not inclusive in its year-round strategy conversation, most employees will not have enough context to weigh in on strategy in the first place, which is its own problem. **If they don't understand enough to set strategy, they probably don't know enough to make strategically advantageous decisions daily.** That problem is worth fixing, but you cannot fix it with a one-time listening session or brainstorming exercise.

ANALYSES OF ORGANIZATIONAL EFFECTIVENESS

Leadership Effectiveness

Much of organizational effectiveness comes down to how effectively leaders work together. Bringing data to this topic via observations and understanding how others in the organization experience leaders can help identify the most impactful opportunities for improvement. The polar graph in Figure A6 compares how leaders rated their performance and how others rated the leaders.

Organizational Capabilities: Today v. Tomorrow

An important part of strategic success is coherently matching organizational capabilities to intended outcomes. As the organization considers updating its strategy, it may need a new understanding of what capabilities are most important going forward. The analysis shown in Figure A7 can bring insight to that question.

ANALYSES OF WHAT'S HAPPENING OUTSIDE OF THE ORGANIZATION

The value of doing a deep analysis of the external environment is situation-specific. It is likely more important when there are significant changes coming due to technology or government policy that could greatly alter clients' needs and organizations' ability to serve them.

Some of these dynamics should be evident when your team identifies its strategic situation and from external stakeholder conversations. Reviewing industry reports can also be a good source of information for the strategy effort.

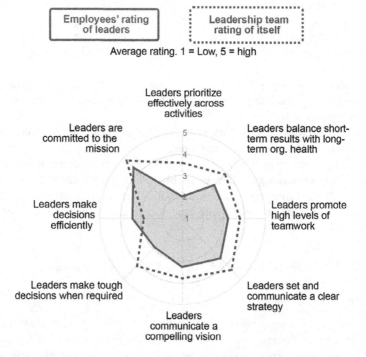

Figure A6 Employee and Leader Ratings of Leadership Effectiveness

Future Capability Needs Exceed Current Capabilities
Average rating among senior leaders

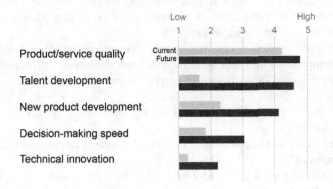

Current Capabilities Exceed Future Capability Needs
Average rating among senior leaders

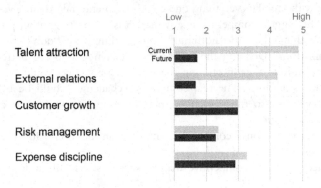

Figure A7 Leader Ratings of Organizational Capabilities

The relevant questions for strategy development include:

- What competitive forces does the industry as a whole face?
- Is the industry increasing or decreasing in size? What is causing that to happen?
- Who from outside of our industry is solving similar customer problems? (Those may be competitors.)

WATCH OUT: COMPETITIVE ANALYSIS

Competitive analysis can often go wrong because "competition" is sometimes incorrectly defined as those organizations offering products or services like yours. This is a supplier-centered view of competition.

Instead, competition should be defined through the lens of stakeholders—e. g., clients, employees, donors, elected officials, key partners—who must choose your organization over others. In that sense, it's customer-centered. Using this framing, the set of competitors is whatever *else* those stakeholders will give their time, money, attention, and effort to.

For example, a supplier-centered competitive analysis would indicate that Tesla is competing with other auto manufacturers. However, a customer-centered analysis would show that their competitors probably also include:

- Low gas prices ("Why switch from my current car if gas is pretty affordable?")
- Other forms of transportation ("I don't need a car. I can just walk or take the subway.")
- Going nowhere ("Do I need a new car at all if I'm working from home most of the time?")

Similarly, Netflix isn't just competing with Hulu, Max, and Paramount+. It's competing with literally everything one could do to entertain themselves.

Finally, the biggest competitor in any market is often not another provider. Instead, it's things like "do nothing," "buy nothing," or "don't donate to *any* organization." Defining the competitive challenge as being better than other organizations already offering the product or service would be a mistake in these situations. The real competitive challenge would be bringing additional people into the market or, better, competing with their current choice of *do nothing*.

For all those reasons, competitive analysis can be tricky for nonprofit organizations.

If you decide to do a competitive analysis, success starts with understanding:

1 *Why are people choosing our product or service?*
2 *What are they choosing over us (including "do nothing"), and in what circumstances?*

Those questions center the competitive analysis on stakeholders' decision-making, enabling you to identify the real competitors and the most important dimensions of the competition.

For example, having the highest service quality or the demonstrably best results may matter in the competition for foundation grants, where program officers will study this data closely and seek to justify their grant proposals based on that information.

However, individual donors usually do not make their decisions logically and deliberately, so competition for them may rest on different organizational capabilities—like branding, storytelling, and generating emotional responses.

Notes

1 Fred Reichheld, Darci Darnell, and Maureen Burns, *Winning on Purpose: The Unbeatable Strategy of Loving Customers* (Boston, MA: Harvard Business Review Press, 2021), 39, e-book.
2 Amy Edmondson, *The Fearless Organization: Creating Psychological Safety in the Workplace for Learning, Innovation, and Growth* (Hoboken, NJ: Wiley, 2019), xvi, e-book.
3 Ibid, 20.
4 "Gallup's Q12 Employee Engagement Survey—Gallup." Gallup.com, September 16, 2022, www.gallup.com/workplace/356063/gallup-q12-employee-engagement-survey.aspx.
5 Ella F. Washington, Ellyn Maese, and Shane McFeely, "Workplace Engagement and the Glass Ceiling" in Laura Morgan Roberts, Anthony J. Mayo, and David A. Thomas, *Race, Work, and Leadership: New Perspectives on the Black Experience* (Boston, MA: Harvard Business Review Press, 2019), e-book, 120.
6 Frances Frei and Anne Morriss, *Uncommon Service: How to Win by Putting Customers at the Core of Your Business* (Boston, MA: Harvard Business Review Press, 2012), 89, e-book.

References

Amy Edmondson, *The Fearless Organization: Creating Psychological Safety in the Workplace for Learning, Innovation, and Growth* (Hoboken, NJ: Wiley, 2019), xvi, e-book.
Frances Frei and Anne Morriss, *Uncommon Service: How to Win by Putting Customers at the Core of Your Business* (Boston, MA: Harvard Business Review Press, 2012), 89, e-book.
"Gallup's Q12 Employee Engagement Survey—Gallup." Gallup.com, September 16, 2022, www.gallup.com/workplace/356063/gallup-q12-employee-engagement-survey.aspx.
Fred Reichheld, Darci Darnell, and Maureen Burns, *Winning on Purpose: The Unbeatable Strategy of Loving Customers* (Boston, MA: Harvard Business Review Press, 2021), 39, e-book.
Ella F. Washington, Ellyn Maese, and Shane McFeely, "Workplace Engagement and the Glass Ceiling." In Laura Morgan Roberts, Anthony J. Mayo, and David A. Thomas, *Race, Work, and Leadership: New Perspectives on the Black Experience* (Boston, MA: Harvard Business Review Press, 2019), 120, e- book.

Designing Your Organization's Strategy System. A Step-By-Step Guide

This Appendix expands upon the discussion of the third element of Strategic FUEL in Chapter 7 and will walk through creating a system that works for your organization. There are four steps to the design process, each of which has sub-steps:

1 Identify the Right Questions to Ask
2 Assess the Current State
3 Identify Experiments to Address the Most Important Gaps
4 Identify the Right Data

It's essential to address these in order.

STEP 1: IDENTIFY THE RIGHT QUESTIONS TO ASK

An effective set of strategic routines helps the organization **evolve** and **learn** continuously. This keeps the strategy relevant to the organization's evolving situation rather than letting it calcify.

But to learn and evolve, the organization must first define "success." The mission and strategy of the organization should provide that definition. And with the success definition as the foundation, the questions the team should ask should:

1 Inform how well the organization is performing relative to the success definition; and,
2 Identify the most important areas and means for improvement.

On your own or as a team, create a list of questions that will address those areas. Here are some questions to prime that thinking.
   On organizational performance:

• How effectively are we achieving the most important outcomes for our mission?

- How satisfied are the people we serve with what we offer?
- How effectively are we delivering an employee and volunteer experience that attracts and retains committed and talented people?
- How effectively are we resourcing the organization?
- How well are we delivering on the success metrics critical partners, supporters, and funders use to evaluate our success?

On strategic progress:

- What's most essential for us to improve in the near term? (This is the strategy.) What would signal that we are making that progress?
- How effectively are we addressing long-term drivers of success?

Don't Jump Prematurely to Metrics!

It can be tempting to jump immediately to success metrics rather than starting with the questions, but that is a mistake. Why? First, numbers do not tell the whole story.

For example, if your organization is a food pantry, you can count the number of people served as a success metric. But is an increase in that number good or bad?

Well, it's good if the organization finds new ways to reach more people or the people you serve are so satisfied that they refer others they know who need support. Those are signs the organization is performing well. But it would NOT be good to see an increase in people served if it results from sharply increased needs in the community.

This example shows that the metric may not tell you anything about the organization's performance. The only way to know what the data means is to know what question it is intended to answer. That is why it is worth starting with the questions.

This dynamic also happens with financial data. For example, creating a dashboard with, say, Year-to-Date Fundraising Revenue is easy. That is important information. However, if the *most* important question is, *Is our fundraising high enough to meet our expenses?* Or *Is our fundraising sufficient to meet our goal of increasing cash reserves by $2M?*, the data you would want on the dashboard would be different.

Again, this is why starting with questions rather than metrics helps ensure performance conversations address the most critical aspects of strategy. (We'll talk about this later, but it is also helpful to include the questions on whatever data dashboards you create so that the meaning does not get lost.)

Another reason to start with questions rather than metrics is that not every important aspect of organizational performance is quantifiable—or easily quantified regularly. For example, the leadership team may want to ask questions like:

- Are we sparking joy in our students?
- Are we creating more justice in the world?
- Is our culture as action-oriented as we need it to be?

There's no data that will answer those questions precisely. And even if there were, you probably would not be able to get data that helps you assess if the organization is improving on a week-to-week or month-to-month basis.

However, if those are important questions for the strategy, having them front and center in the team's performance conversation is still worthwhile.

A personal example. In the annual strategy retreat my wife and I hold, we ask two important questions about our finances: *Do our finances support our values?* and *Are we comfortable with our situation and the plan?*

There are metrics in other areas—e.g., savings rate and progress to retirement goals—but for questions about our feelings on the finances, the data we use for analysis is "How much do you agree?" But that is enough to spark a conversation that can lead to changes in strategy.

Focusing back on organizations, the process of articulating the questions is a valuable exercise for generating alignment among the team about what good performance looks like. That alignment is critical to creating a culture of accountability for the results. It is far easier to push the team to deliver success if they have already agreed to the definition of success.

STEP 2: ASSESS THE CURRENT STATE

This exercise aims to identify where, if at all, the questions you specified in the previous step are currently being discussed. I describe it here as a solo exercise, but you can do it with a team.

Step 2A: Create a Map of Current Forums

Down the left of a sheet of paper—or the first column of a spreadsheet—list all of the questions you identified in the previous step.

Create a second column to list the forums—i.e., when and where—the team currently addresses each question. Forums can include meetings and informal communication channels, like a team chat, text message forum, or seeing each other in the hallways.

The key here is to hold a high bar. For example, it may be tempting to say, "We discuss client feedback in our leadership team meetings." But if that conversation is haphazard, shallow, or does not lead to action, the answer might be, "We're not discussing it today."

Question	Where and when we answer it today	Effectiveness rating
1.		
2.		
3.		
4.		
5.		
6.		

Figure B1 Analysis of Current Forums

Step 2B: Assess the Conversations

In a third column, rate the effectiveness of the conversation about each question on a scale of 1 to 5, where 1 signifies a shallow or non-existent treatment of it, and 5 indicates a robust, data-informed, action-oriented conversation.

One option to engage the team is to have them rate the conversations on each question. Another way to engage them is to allocate five to ten minutes in the following instances of the critical meetings or forums to solicit feedback from participants. This can be in the form of an open discussion (e.g., "What is one thing we can do to make this meeting more effective?"), or a short survey that you ask them to fill out right then. While the top leader may unilaterally implement changes to routines, soliciting the perspectives of those participating in the routine can yield new ideas and greater buy-in to the solutions.

Step 2C: Identify and Prioritize Opportunities for Improvement

Ask yourself or the team these questions:

- How can we make those forums/conversations more effective?
- How can we make those forums/conversations more action-oriented and inclusive?

STEP 3: IDENTIFY EXPERIMENTS TO ADDRESS THE MOST IMPORTANT GAPS

The previous step should help you (and the team) identify the most important ways to improve your strategic conversation. Now, you'll have to decide how to proceed. There's no single correct answer. Some advice:

Prioritize Efforts

It's hard to drive change all at once. So, use the data to align the team around the most important places to start.

Start with What Exists

People will push back if you propose a whole new set of meetings, but there's usually a lot of openness to efforts to make existing meetings more effective.

Tactically, you can use the feedback you gather to propose the following for each of the prioritized routines/forums:

- Objective(s)
- Cadence
- Agenda
- Participants
- Participant expectations (e.g., what information, perspectives, and mind-sets are required from participants to achieve the objectives).

Use the Language of "Experiments"

In the next instance of the routine, engage the participants in your proposal. The goal is to get everyone to agree (at minimum) to experiment with the new routine design.

That agreement sets the stage for continued conversation and refinement of the routine. For example, once everyone agrees to "We need to focus on the highest priority topics and make faster decisions in this meeting," you can continually ask, "Are we accomplishing this?"

That loop is what helps create the desired change over time.

Just Get Started

Don't wait to have the perfect plan. It does not exist!

This effort is about **building the muscles** to have robust conversations. Because that takes time, the effort should start as soon as possible. In the next step, we'll talk about adding data to the conversation, but even this is unnecessary to get the ball rolling.

STEP 4: IDENTIFY THE RIGHT DATA

The previous steps were about creating a set of strategic conversations. Supporting those conversations with data is the last step. It should come last partly because it is often the hardest one.

Step 4A: Identify the Data

For each strategy and performance question, the core question is: What information would give us the best indicator of success or progress?

Step 4B: Assess Data Availability

If you are building the system from scratch, you may not have all the data currently available. However, now is not the time to launch a considerable effort to collect all the data. Instead, you want to start with what's available and build out the system as you go.

Note: If the data is unavailable, it could be worth examining why. For example, the data might not be available because front-line staff do not find the data helpful to collect or analyze. That could be a sign that those staff think of success differently than senior leaders—an opportunity for further conversation. Similarly, data unavailability may signal issues with technology systems that could be worth solving.

Step 4C: Prioritize Efforts to Build Data Over Time

The most important thing is that the team is having the conversation regularly. It's OK if the first conversations and the first versions of the dashboards include placeholders like "Forthcoming" or "Data TBD."

Moreover, even with a mature dashboard and data system, the team would not need to update every measure monthly. For example, some data might be collected semiannually or annually—e.g., extensive employee surveys, collecting formal feedback from clients and external stakeholders.

Still, it's worth having those items on the dashboard because qualitative assessments (e.g., "what we've been hearing from clients lately is …") can lead to important insights and action between formal data collection efforts. One reason it is helpful to set up your new cadence first is that it creates a timeline for filling in the data gaps over time.

Tips on Getting Started

1 Don't worry (for now) about creating a "dashboard."

That may be the final format, but if you push that as the specific visual format for all of the data, it can distract from the core exercise of identifying the data to answer the strategy questions. As you get started, eliminate the distraction of formatting. If the final product is just a list of data in a document but supports a robust strategic conversation, that is a win!

2 The best data could be stated in "ratio" form.

The best data is explicitly *relative* to something else. For example, knowing year-to-date revenue is helpful, but it may be more informative to view it relative to last year, relative to the budget for this year, or relative to year-to-date expenses.

Or, consider the number of people the organization serves. Is the most useful data relative to last month, relative to the commitments the organization has made to funders, or something else? The only way to know the right approach is to develop the metrics based on the question you're trying to answer.

The guidance here is not necessarily to show the data as a ratio—indeed, that can be confusing. Instead, it is a nudge to make the dashboard as clear as possible. For example:

- Labeling the data clearly. There should be no confusion about what the data is.
- Showing the reference point—e.g., the goal, the same metric from the previous month/year/quarter—immediately next to the latest data
- Using plain language so that people who are unfamiliar with the data (or are less data-fluent) can easily interpret what the data means

3 Don't forget external reporting, but don't let it drive the effort.

Creating strategic management routines nudges the organization to develop infrastructure for easy, regular reporting of data you need for grant reports, compliance, and annual reports. Even if some of this data is not part of your organization's mission success definition, including the data in regular reporting is helpful because it keeps teams on track to deliver it. That is, it helps you avoid the rush to assemble these reports when they are due.

TOOLS TO SUPPORT YOUR NEW ORGANIZATIONAL ROUTINES

Bring Strategy Visuals into Your Team's Space—and Conversation

Visualization is a critical part of the Toyota Production System, widely considered one of the most effective manufacturing processes. In the book *The Toyota Way*, Jeffrey Liker writes, "The Toyota Way recognizes that visual management complements humans because we are visually, tactilely, and audibly oriented. And the best visual indicators are right at the worksite, where they can jump out at you and clearly indicate by sound, sight, and feel the standard and any deviation from the standard."[1]

The visual indicators that Liker describes can be anything from intricate data dashboards that show the status of every part of the system to having a workspace that is tidy enough that you can readily see what is out of place or missing. Put simply, when things are visual, it is easier to see opportunities for improvement.

But while the Toyota Production System was built to make physical goods, it is centered on the *human process* of spotting opportunities, collaboratively solving problems, and taking action. The principles are relevant for many environments.

Liker indicates that "the best visual indicators are right at the worksite." For many teams at Toyota, this means printing charts and graphs with performance data and making them accessible to everyone. That puts performance data in the middle of the conversation. Liker describes a course Ichiro Suzuki, the chief engineer of the first Lexus, taught right before his retirement: "[Suzuki] also pointed out that 'using an electronic monitor does not work if only one person uses that information. Visual management charts must allow for communication and sharing.'"[2]

Earlier, I mentioned the CEO Shannon Byrne Susko and how her teams created "strategy pictures." Her teams also brought those pictures into their workspace. The strategic pictures were literally on the walls. She writes, "Pictures were always in front of us, at every meeting. When we shared pictures as a team, people could tell right away what we were talking about. They could see whether something had changed, internally or externally, since the previous meeting."[3]

Because they were accessible, the pictures could be referred to *and edited* as the team learned—either in their routine interactions or formal strategic check-ins on a monthly or quarterly cadence. That's Strategic FUEL.

Designing Effective Dashboards

I loooooove a great data dashboard. I have looked at exceptionally well-designed dashboards and said, without irony, "That's sexy."

Perhaps because of this interest, I'm usually underwhelmed when seeing organizations' dashboards. Most of those I have seen are poorly designed or used in a suboptimal way. The aspiration is good—figuring out how to synthesize the most important data and drive better decisions—but the intended outcome is often not achieved.

The following principles can make these tools more effective.

Principle 1: Great dashboards answer specific, meaningful questions

Too often, leaders think creating a dashboard means simply putting all the information in one place. But that's not a dashboard; that's a report. A great dashboard does not just provide data. It answers specific questions.

Your monthly bank statement is an example of this distinction. The bank statement reports how much money is in each of your accounts.

However, the most *meaningful* questions about your finances might be: *Do I have enough in the checking account I use for paying bills to cover next month's bills?* Or *Is my rainy day savings account enough to cover six months' expenses?*

Because the bank statement provides information rather than answering the most important questions, it's a report rather than a dashboard.

In organizations, a view that provides just the revenue and expense data is a report. A view that answers, *Are we on track to reach our revenue goal?* or, *How much of our expense reduction targets have been realized to date?* is likely a dashboard.

The first step in creating a great dashboard is clarity in what questions you want it to answer for you. As you can see from these analogies, the questions themselves dictate what data is most meaningful.

In terms of design, I'm a fan of putting the questions directly in the dashboard for clarity.

For example, in creating a health dashboard for myself, I might put "change in weight over the past month" as one of the measures. This is probably better than just reporting my current weight. But if I showed it to someone else without context, they might ask: *Are you trying to lose weight or gain weight? How much? By when? For what reason?* Putting the meaningful question on the dashboard eliminates confusion.

This may seem trivial. It's easy to think everyone will know what you're discussing. But the reminder is helpful for your boss or your board who do not think about your work every day. The reminder is even beneficial for your team, as they can sometimes lose track of the overarching goals.

The final reason to use meaningful questions as the foundation of dashboards is that qualitative judgments may best answer the most important questions. For example: *How effective is our organization? How robust is our new product pipeline?*

When you start with data as the framing, the dashboard can be biased toward those things we can measure today and leave out essential elements of the strategy.

Even having blank spaces for "we can't measure this yet" is helpful to see!

Principle 2: Great dashboards distinguish between strategy and monitoring

To understand the distinction, consider the difference between your car dashboard's fuel (or battery) gauge and the navigation map. The fuel gauge is essential, but you only want to know that it's above a certain level. The gauge goes up and down, but you're not actively *trying* to make it be at a certain level. On the other hand, the navigation map describes where you want to go and provides information about how well you are progressing toward that destination.

That represents the difference between a monitoring dashboard and a strategy one. The best dashboards I've seen separate strategy metrics from monitoring metrics.

This is part of clarifying the meaningful questions. For the strategy metrics, the questions are, "Are we making progress?" For the monitoring metrics, the questions are more like, "Is there a problem we don't know about?"

Principle 3: Great dashboards should be management tools, not just reporting tools

Put another way, great dashboards should be what leaders use day-to-day to run the organization. This is the ultimate test of relevance.

For example, imagine asking someone, "How are we doing on customer retention?" If they cannot immediately show you on their day-to-day dashboard or do not have the data memorized, here's what is likely the case:

- You're not on the same page about how important customer retention is or have a different logic about how the business works.
- The person is not actively managing customer retention, even though you believe it's strategically important.
- There is no mechanism to measure customer retention effectively.

In all cases, this is evidence of a lack of strategic alignment and should trigger a helpful two-way conversation about the work.

In practice, many dashboards are only created because the board or senior leader requests a synthesized view of what's happening. In those cases, a helpful question when a dashboard is presented to you is: Which data do you look at daily, and which is just generated for this meeting?

There's another super practical reason to ensure that the dashboard is used as a management tool: If the data in the dashboard is not generated in the normal flow of work, it becomes a pain to update. That makes it more likely that the dashboard will be of lower quality and that the effort to create it will be less sustainable.

Principle 4: Great dashboards should spark the right conversations

Imagine getting a report card from school and never talking with your parents about it. This was my experience growing up. Because I was ... well, a nerd who got all Grade As, my dad would never ask questions about my report card. It took about thirty seconds for him to review it, and we moved on. But that is not a great practice in organizations!

To achieve their highest and best use, dashboards should exist to support effective strategy conversations.

Step one in achieving this outcome is orienting the dashboard to answer meaningful questions. When the dashboard reflects the strategy, it can be a tool for strategic discussion.

The second step is to design the discussions around the dashboard to be most effective. Tactically, the agenda item shouldn't be "Review the dashboard." Instead, it should be "Review the organization's impact and progress, using the dashboard to support that conversation."

In the most effective routines, there is a clear expectation that the person presenting the dashboard—the person responsible for moving the data on it—comes to the meeting with:

- A clear perspective on what is most important
- The next-level analysis already complete (e.g., a deeper dive on those things that are off-track or surprising)
- A proposal for what they will do next
- Requests for the group (e.g., questions they need help answering, tactical support)

That's what good looks like.

This is also why a dashboard must serve as a management tool, not just a reporting tool. If it reflects how they do the job daily, the leader is much more likely to feel ownership over the results and think about how to move forward.

Principle 5: Great dashboards maximize the signal-to-noise ratio

An excellent example of a high signal-to-noise indicator is your car's Check Engine light. It's just one symbol, and you know exactly what to do when it's on—check the engine!

Now imagine that instead of one symbol, the Check Engine light was replaced by a readout of every metric used to calculate whether the engine has a problem. It would be overwhelming, confusing, and distracting. This is poor signal-to-noise.

The takeaway: Dashboards should be powered by data, but they should not necessarily *have* all the data. When the Check Engine light is on, that is the cue to to go deeper and show more about what is happening. Otherwise, the details are not helpful.

The book *Universal Principles of Design* provides some helpful tips on how to increase the signal-to-noise ratio of your dashboard: "Maximizing signal means clearly communicating information with minimal degradation. Signal degradation occurs when information is presented inefficiently: unclear writing, inappropriate graphs, or ambiguous icons and labels."[4]

And: "Minimizing noise means removing unnecessary elements, and minimizing the expression of necessary elements. It is important to realize that every unnecessary data item, graphic, line, or symbol steals attention away from relevant elements."[5]

Here's a great test of whether the signal-to-noise ratio is right: Can you see the most important takeaways at a glance? If not, there's room to improve the dashboard design.

Your dashboards might not reach "sexy" level, but if they meet these principles, I bet they will be more helpful!

Notes

1 Jeffrey K. Liker, *The Toyota Way: 14 Management Principles from the World's Greatest Manufacturer* (McGraw Hill, 2021), 156, e-book.
2 Ibid.
3 Shannon Byrne Susko, *3HAG Way: The Strategic Execution System that Ensures Your Strategy is Not a Wild-Ass-Guess!* (Shannon Byrne Susko, 2018), 153, e-book.
4 William Lidwell, Kritina Holden, and Jill Butler, *Universal Principles of Design* (Beverly, MA: Rockport Publishers, 2010), 224.
5 Ibid.

References

Shannon Byrne Susko, *3HAG Way: The Strategic Execution System that Ensures Your Strategy is Not a Wild-Ass-Guess!* (Shannon Byrne Susko, 2018), 153, e-book.
William Lidwell, Kritina Holden, and Jill Butler, *Universal Principles of Design* (Beverly, MA: Rockport Publishers, 2010), 224.
Jeffrey K. Liker, *The Toyota Way: 14 Management Principles from the World's Greatest Manufacturer* (McGraw Hill, 2021), 156, e-book.

More Resources and Taking Action

Download the Bonus Resources

Throughout the book, there were several references to the Bonus Resources. You can download all of them from the book website. In the Bonus Resources, you'll find:

- The Four Elements of Strategic FUEL: How Does Your Organization Currently Stack Up?
- Strategic Planning Objectives and Agreement Template
- Participant Planner
- Creating an Effective Strategy Working Group
- Tiger Team Charter Proposal
- What to Read to Learn More About Strategy

www.thrivestreetadvisors.com/strategic-fuel-for-nonprofits

I'd Love to Hear Your Story!

First, thanks for reading the book! I know your time and attention are valuable resources. If you've enjoyed the book, please leave a review on Amazon or wherever you made your purchase. Those reviews help others find the book.

If you have used any of the tools in this book, please visit our website and let me know how they impacted your organization!

Do You Need More Help?

The intention of this book was to give you the tools to lead an effective strategic planning process. However, covering every topic or all possible nuances is hard. If you have questions, please visit our website (www.thrivestreetadvisors.com/strategic-fuel-for-nonprofits).

Of course, we also help organizations do this work. You can find out how we do this on Thrive Street's website (www.thrivestreetadvisors.com/strategy).

Index

Printed in the United States
by Baker & Taylor Publisher Services